BIG BRASS BALLS:

THE "HIGH-FUNCTIONING SOCIOPATH'S BLUEPRINT" THAT REMOVES ALL FEAR, ERASES ALL DOUBT, AND COMMANDS EFFORTLESS SUCCESS

RAYMOND MARYLOWE

First edition: 12th November 2025

Copyright ©2025 Raymond Marylowe

All rights reserved. No part of this book may be reproduced, distributed, or transmitted in any form or by any means, including photocopying, recording, or other electronic or mechanical methods, without the prior written permission of the author, except in the case of brief quotations embodied in critical reviews and certain other noncommercial uses permitted by copyright law.

Published by / Publié par
Scientia Publishing (Éditions Scientia)
Rue Meurein, 59800 Lille, France

ISBN: 978-1-7642520-4-1 (Paperback)
ISBN: 978-1-7642520-5-8 (Hardcover)

This is a work of fiction. Names, characters, places, and incidents are either products of the author's imagination or are used fictitiously. Any resemblance to actual persons, living or dead, or actual events is purely coincidental.

Library of Congress Cataloging-in-Publication data available upon request from the publisher.

PROFESSOR Raymond Marylowe is an Associate Professor in Theoretical Physics at Imperial College London, with an h-index of 60,000. He is also the author of the bestseller, *The Physicist Detective vs. the Criminal Defense Lawyer.*

Foreword By An Obsessed Reader

I'd just finished reading *The Physicist Detective vs. the Criminal Defense Lawyer,* and I had a thousand questions about Raymond Marylowe. The question that kept screaming in my head was simple: is this guy for real?

It was incredible. Who the **** was this guy? Who the **** thinks like this? Initially, the book felt like a clear parody. But the further you got into it, the more you realized it was a Trojan horse. It was something else entirely smuggled in under the disguise of a joke. Because I've never encountered a mind that works like this.

I reached out to Marylowe asking for permission to compile his "lessons"—his most unhinged and hilarious insights—into a PDF. Then I waited.

A week later, he replied. He thanked me for the idea, and, of course, said he'd already stolen the idea and made a book out of it. But he invited me to write this foreword.

Of course he did. What the hell did I expect?

And the book you're holding is exactly what I expected. It's the "Greatest Hits" compilation of his philosophy, packaged up and ready to go. It's a perfect distillation of the Physicist Detective's mind, plus several brand new chapters.

This part had me genuinely laughing out loud, when he mentioned in passing American Psycho.

"It's clear to me the writer isn't a real sociopath, and doesn't even live or work in the sociopath circle, and really he's just writing things he knew nothing about."

This captures my thoughts perfectly. Professor Raymond Marylowe is a "high-functioning sociopath", but isn't the idealized, fictional version that they show you on TV. Like they show you a BBC Sherlock, a Tyler Durden, or a Patrick Bateman. But they're all static. They never explain why the character is the way they are, it's just "he's born that way."

But the Professor is not a born sociopath. He is a **philosopher of sociopathy**. No, scratch that. He's a **missionary of sociopathy**. The story meticulously details his internal operating system and, accidentally or intentionally, teaches you how to adopt it through his lessons. The original book, and now this compilation, might as well be a **blueprint for sociopathy**. And the joke is just the delivery system for the "sociopath blueprint".

What's truly surprising is **how frighteningly coherent Raymond Marylowe's philosophy is.** It's not a collection of clever ideas or the ramblings of a madman. It's an entire operating system built from scratch to eliminate guilt, fear, hesitation. Every point is connected to other points. If it's a joke, it's the most elaborate joke ever.

And even having written this foreword, I still don't know if he's serious or not.

—Francis "Ice" Bennett

Introduction by Professor Raymond Marylowe

Well done for picking up this book! So you've realized that the only way to achieve any sort of success is to grow a pair. And you're right! Allow me, with a physicist's precision, to break down the formula for success once and for all for you:

Success is 1% talent, 1% hard work, 1% luck, and the rest is all about audacity.

That's why all the heroes are from Gryffindor, see?

Audacity is not "courage". A typical man needs to psych himself up, or have a few drinks, then **maybe** he'd manage a few moments of courage here and there. These moments become the highlights of his life, and he pats himself on the back feeling good about overcoming his fear.

But really, he's weak. Think about it, "courage" means you still feel fear. Otherwise you wouldn't need courage. You'd just go ahead and do it!

Why don't most people just "do it"? Because they walk

through life dragging a massive sack of 100-pound boulders that is their emotional baggage: self-doubt, insecurities, societal nonsense. All of these are based on fear.

By the way, that's why motivation doesn't work. Most motivation advice is about "adding" things: more routines, more systems, more goals and tricks. But it ignores the boulders you're already carrying!

Imagine having no fear. Then you wouldn't even need courage. You wouldn't even need confidence. You'd just act and win, effortlessly, because there'll be nothing holding you back. Easier said than done, right? But I'm going to teach you the one and only way to completely remove all fear.

By the way, this is why this book works very fast, in days to weeks. Because it's always quicker and easier to "remove" than to "develop". So forget about building confidence or courage. Focus on **removing fear**.

After you finish this book, you'll finally get rid of that sack of boulders and will be able to walk lightly. If you're dragging anything with you, it'll be your enormous Big Brass Balls. But they won't slow you down. Instead, they will energize you. Because they're not literal balls, because ladies can have them too!

How to remove fear?

They say all fear comes from the unknown, it's true. The best way to remove fear is this: I'm going to remove the unknown for you. **I'm going to show you the truth of the world!**

That's right. This book isn't about some superficial motivation, or some inspirational quotes that stop working after

INTRODUCTION BY PROFESSOR RAYMOND MARYLOWE

a day or two... No. This book... is truly scary... because it's dangerous. I can't stress how dangerous it is! Because once you see the truth? **You can never unsee it!** You can never go back to who you were before, even if you want to. For a lot of people, even this journey is too scary for them. But then they can never hope to have the Brass Balls to begin with.

But what is "truth" anyway?

I know what you're thinking, *"Alright, Professor, so you promise to tell me the 'truth'. But everyone claims they know the truth. How do I know this time is different?"*

Ah, yes. So people have been lying to you your entire life, and you believed in their B.S. That's what got you so stuck in the first place. Well, I never had this problem, do you know why? Because I derived everything I know from first principles!

Listen, if you're reading this book, you're probably a **guy**, you probably even **consider yourself smart**, which means your mind operates **more on logic than emotion.** In that case, **you need to have a coherent worldview built from the ground up, with first principles and with logic.** No other book on the planet has done it, but I'm going to do it for you.

As you know, I'm a theoretical physicist. In theoretical physics, everything in the universe can be explained by two equations, Einstein field equation and Standard Model. From these two equations, you can deduce and calculate everything you want to know about in the entire world. Every single thing!

Still, physicists aren't happy about it. We don't want two equations, we want one single master equation, The Theory of Everything. We always look for the **simplest explanation**, because we know **the truth is always simple.**

So that's what I'm going to do. We're going to start with a couple of axioms, and **derive the whole world for you.** They say human behaviors are complicated and messier than physics. But really, "they" are just too dumb to figure it out. The reality is that the world is actually very simple!

By the way, this is the reason this book is so small. It's intentional, so you can fit the book into your coat pocket, and keep it close to your heart. I want you to be constantly reminded of it and read it whenever you can. Read it multiple times until the lessons truly internalize! Alright, enough chit-chat, let's get started!

Contents

Foreword By An Obsessed Reader iii

Introduction By Professor Raymond Marylowe v
    But what is "truth" anyway? vii

1 The Majority Is Always Wrong   3
    I can prove the majority is wrong when it comes to wealth 3
    I can prove the majority is wrong when it comes to love and relationships 4
    I can prove the majority is wrong when it comes to health 4
    "The Mediocre Majority lead lives of muted desperation" 4
    The majority of the experts are idiots 5
    Success is easy… just do the opposite of what they tell you 6
    Shameless is your superpower 7

2 What Is A Human?   9
    How to deal with Homer? 10

	What's the point of the rules, really?	13
	What are rules, really?	14
3	No Such Thing As Self-Doubt, Only Hypocrisy	19
	Anything in "self-help" and psychology is full of traps	22
	Some traps are very insidious	23
	How to liberate yourself from traps	25
	Reject all psychological labels	27
	The tale of Mensa society—a society of morons...	28
4	Psychology Is An Unfalsifiable Pseudo-Science	29
	1. Clinical psychology is not falsifiable	29
	2. Psychology is not reproducible	32
	3. Data can be easily manipulated	33
	4. Clinical psychology is all about self-reporting	34
	5. Statistics cannot describe individuals . . .	34
	6. Mental illnesses do not exist by definition .	36
	Science has nothing to do with "truth"	37
5	God Alone Can Judge	39
	Erase the lies of "divine punishment" or "karmic justice"	40
	Erase the lies of "deserving" and "fairness" . .	41
	Erase the lies of "integrity" and "dignity" . . .	42
	Erase the lie of "truth"	44
	Erase the lies of "good" and "bad"	45
	"Good" and "bad" depends on perspectives .	48
	"Good" and "bad" change depending on where you are	49

Contents

    "Good" and "bad" really means "natural" and
    "unnatural" 50
    But if nothing is real, what can we believe in?   52

6 What Can You Believe In? (According To The Criminal Defense Lawyer)   53
    The Olympus Group case 54
    The Senator has a dream 59
    The law isn't about justice 61

7 Justice Is Winning (According To The Criminal Defense Lawyer)   65
    Master the system 66
    Morality is a disease 68
    What the Senator would've done 69

8 What Can You Believe In, Really?   73
    Live your own truth 75
    You must take full responsibility of your life . 76
    You must become self-reliant 77
    How to respect other people's autonomy . . . 78
    Finally, Embrace Ugliness 79

9 Professor's Practical Q&A Session   83
    "Professor, how do I develop social skills?" . . 83
    "Professor, how do I get people to respect me?" 84
    "Professor, how do I deal with hate?" 84
    "Professor, what if I'm feeling lost in life?" . . 85
    "Professor, how to deal with trauma?" 86
    "Professor, what if I'm addicted and distracted?" 88

    "Professor, can you teach me a good pick-up line?" 89
    "Professor, I found a girlfriend, now what?" . 91
    "Professor, what 'mindset' should I have?" . . 92

10 How To Fix "Paralysis By Analysis" (a.k.a. Stupidity)   95

Afterword   103

11 True Courage vs. Toxic Courage   107

Dedication   111

About The Author   113

Big Brass Balls

1

THE MAJORITY IS ALWAYS WRONG

IF you could take away one thing from this book, just remember this: the majority is always wrong! Always! This is the fundamental axiom!

"But Professor, this sounds like an opinion, not a fact!"

And you're right... I can't prove it in every case. **But I can prove it in a whole lot of cases!**

I can prove the majority is wrong when it comes to wealth

The majority of the people have no money. You already know 10% of the people have 70% of the wealth, most people fight for scraps. It's the worst for millennials and Gen-Z's. According to the feds, about 40% of adults don't have $400 in savings. About 50% can't pull $1,000. And how many do you think are one medical emergency away from bankruptcy? 70%? 80%?

There you have it, **the majority is wrong in terms of money.**

I can prove the majority is wrong when it comes to love and relationships

About 50% of marriages end in divorce, and even for the married ones, not everyone is happy. But that's still not the whole story! Because only about 50% of adults are married in the first place, and another 10% are in a stable relationship.

So really, less than 40% of people are loved and fulfilled. **The majority is wrong in terms of relationships.**

I can prove the majority is wrong when it comes to health

75%+ of adults have at least one chronic disease! A typical U.S. adult spends more than 50% of their life taking at least one prescription drug. Well, maybe it's not all their fault. So let's talk about addictions, which are within their control. Substance abuse and gambling add up to about 30% of the population. Also, most addictions these days are digital, I heard 80–90% of men watch pornography at least weekly!

Clearly, the majority of people are trapped. The majority have bad health and/or have no respect for their health!

"The Mediocre Majority lead lives of muted desperation"

When we say "majority" or "mediocre", we think "average". Not good, not bad, just in the middle.

But really, if you think about it, the "average" life is very bad! What does it look like? You're broke, you're unloved, you're addicted, you and your family might get sick and you can't do anything about it. It's miserable!

If you fear one thing, it shouldn't be the fear of death or fear of judgment... it should be the fear of becoming one of the Mediocre Majority!

* * *

Alright, so we can't trust the general public. Can we trust the experts? Obviously not!

The majority of the experts are idiots

There's the famous "reproducibility crisis" in psychology, and really in all "social sciences". More than 50% of the psychological research cannot be reproduced.

Let me repeat that, **more than 50% of the research is garbage!** You'd be better off flipping a coin!

But you already know social scientists are idiots, that's why they had to become social scientists, because they're incapable of doing anything else. But really, it's not only them, it's **all experts!**

Let's look at finance: More than 50% of the hedge funds lose money, more than 80% under-perform the market.

How could this be? Everyone's saying these experts are legit, so they must be! Look at the glamour of Wall Street, their expertise, their amazing work ethic, their unshakable confidence! They get paid millions! You'd think that finally, here are a group of people who are not complete idiots!

Sadly, reality is often disappointing. Yes… even they… are idiots. Statistics are irrefutable, numbers don't lie. At least, a number like 80% is too conclusive to be a lie.

You might say, *"Wait a minute, but they **are** geniuses. They keep losing money for their clients… yet they still manage to get paid millions? Clearly, they might not be genius bankers… but they're **genius scammers**!"*

Ah, so you think there's some grand conspiracy going on, that the experts are malicious, that they're out there to scam you. Maybe it's true, maybe it's not. But either way, it makes no difference.

But really, you over-estimate them. Think about it, here's a hedge fund manager who dedicated his entire life to understanding the market, who worked like hell to get to where he is, and he considers himself to be the very image of success…

… but he's beat by retired farmer Joe who knows nothing but stocks, who's just buying index funds?

Do you really think the fund manager is happy about it? Do you really think he didn't **want to** beat the farmer? Do you really think he didn't **try** at least once in his life to actually get good at his job?

Oh, of course he tried. He probably even tried his best… he just couldn't win, no matter how hard he tried! Because he's an idiot! Hahaha!

Success is easy… just do the opposite of what they tell you

You haven't realized it yet, but you've just been given the answer to all questions in life. If you ever feel lost, just look at what most other people are doing… and do the opposite!

You're already now in the right direction, guaranteed! And if you're unsure what the "opposite" means, then just stop doing what they're doing.

Here's a foolproof method. If you're ever lost, whether it's in career, in relationships, in business. Just go on social media like Facebook or Reddit, ask your question, and look at the answer with the most likes and upvotes... **and you do the opposite.**

These days it's actually even easier. Just ask AI what to do in a situation—**and do the opposite!** Because AI is already trained on majority opinion!

Because if you follow the advice most people approve of? You're **guaranteed** to become one of them! And if you do the opposite? You literally **cannot** go wrong!

Shameless is your superpower

People who need confidence are weak. You don't need confidence, you just need to remove shame.

In fact, to achieve true success, **you need to be shameless, and delusional, in that order.**

Being delusional is no good by itself! Say if you're delusional but not shameless—that's a miserable existence. You're afraid of people's judgment, but since you're not in touch with reality, you don't even know what they're judging you for. You're imprisoned by a prison of your own making!

If you're shameless but not delusional—now we're getting somewhere! You're a pragmatist who isn't burdened by societal nonsense, you pursue what you know is good for you and you don't let anything hurt you or stop you. You can go far in life!

But if you're both shameless and delusional?! Oh my God, **you're now an invincible and unstoppable force of nature.** I certainly don't know how to stop such a person. Do you?

Some people think "delusional" and "shameless" are "bad" words. But think about it. Delusional according to whom? According to the majority? But they're all stuck. So if they think you're delusional, it means you're on the right track! If they don't think you're delusional, that's when you should be concerned, because it means you're well on your way to becoming one of them!

What about shame? Some people feel shame about climbing their career ladder. But what's there to be ashamed of? Of wanting success? Relationships is another one where people are full of shame. There's the phrase "walk of shame". Many men are ashamed of wanting to chase women. But what are you ashamed of? Of doing God's work?

"Professor, if you're so shameless, why don't you do things like running around naked? The majority is always wrong, right?"

I don't do these things because they're illegal. But maybe going around naked isn't a bad idea! Who knows? Maybe I'll start doing it after they legalize it!

2

What Is A Human?

Okay... but why are the majority always wrong? Let's answer that question. This is undoubtedly the single most important lesson you will ever learn. Because we're going to dive deep into the most fundamental question: what is a human?

You see, fake intellectuals like psychologists and philosophers have been trying to answer the question for centuries, but they still don't understand humans after all these years, because they're too dumb. So allow me to answer it once and for all for you:

Everything you need to understand about a human, is that you must understand **Homer Simpson**. This is someone incredibly lazy, incompetent, and gullible—basically a dumb fat blob.

You're nodding. *"I see, so they're a total waste of space."* But don't hate them for it. Instead, **love them for it!** You can't be happy if you hate the whole world. Instead, be happy you're now better than them!

Now, I'm sure you're asking the obvious follow-up question: *"Alright, Professor. If that is a human, then what is a woman??"*

Glad you asked, because this is important: a woman is not Marge Simpson or Lisa Simpson. **She's also Homer Simpson,** just the female version. Instead of spending hours in front of a TV drinking beer and watching football, she's spending hours eating chocolates and watching cooking shows. Instead of falling for get-rich-quick schemes, she's falling for dumb yoga classes and astrology apps.

How to deal with Homer?

How do we deal with such a person? Yes, they're easy to fool, but it also takes enormous effort just to get them off the couch. They're also very forgetful. So you must take nothing for granted.

As an example, let's talk about gratitude for a second. Of all human emotions, gratitude is the most fleeting. So you must never assume it, you must always invest in it.

Just take me and my fiancée. Her name is Matilda, and she loves me and appreciates me now. And a lot of men might easily fall into the trap of feeling complacent or entitled. But not me. I never take my fiancée's love for granted. Instead, I constantly remind her why she should appreciate me even more and how much she's indebted to me. Similarly, you must constantly remind people of your brilliance, your greatness, and your value. Don't be subtle about it. Do you really think Homer understands subtlety?

If you want a model, just look at Donald Trump. He gets it. Another interesting thing about Trump is how he basically speaks like a 10-year-old. Some people make fun of him, saying "Trump must be a simpleton with the intellect of a 10-year-old."

But that's not quite right. Because here's the thing: he's not speaking like a 10-year-old because he's a 10-year-old simpleton... he's speaking like a 10-year-old because **he's treating all of you like 10-year-old simpletons!** Because he understands the lesson I just taught you!

Now you might be saying, *"But wait a minute... The people in charge are treating me like Homer? But I don't want to be Homer! How do I escape?"*

Ah, but it doesn't matter. Why does it matter? The important part is to figure out how to control the Homers of this world. Then you automatically "escape"! You're either one of us over here, or one of them over there. You can't be both at the same time!

From now on, start holding yourself to a different, higher calling than everyone else.

As an example, you can shame others for their ambitions, but you must be shameless yourself. You can push their boundaries, but you must have impenetrable boundaries yourself. You can impose rules on others, but you must ignore rules yourself.

As an example of the example, I'm sure you've heard of the "half-your-age-plus-seven" rule. Which says you should only date someone who is older than half your age plus seven.

But what happens if you break this rule? What consequences do you suffer? What punishment does society have in store for you?

Well, I happened to have broken this rule with Matilda, who is about a decade younger than me, and I can tell you what happens. If you break the "half-your-age-plus-seven" rule... **society gives you another rule!** It's called the "campsite rule". This one says that if you're dating someone significantly younger, that's fine. You just need to leave her better than you found her!

So it's a good thing I'm not actually breaking societal rules, right?

... But wait a minute. **Do you see a problem here?**

Think about it: I broke a rule, and how does society respond? By giving me another rule! Just in case I broke the first one! Then what's the point of the first rule to begin with?

And in any case, I already broke the first rule, which means I don't care about rules. What makes you think I'd follow the second one? So even the second rule is pointless. Both rules are pointless!

Well, you might think the point was to "prevent young vulnerable women/old vulnerable men from being exploited." But neither is true. If that were the intention, they wouldn't make it a rule, they'd make it a law. And they'd punish you for breaking it.

For example, my fiancée had me sign a prenup to say I can't cheat on her, otherwise she gets all my assets (long story, I won't get into it). That—alright, she wins that round, or so she thinks. But I had to follow that only because it's a law. It's written on a piece of paper, and so it's real. But what about rules? Most people think rules are real, but they're not real!

Because there's never any punishment. If anything, you're rewarded for breaking them. That tells you they were never meant to be enforced, they were meant to be broken. And the reason society gives me another rule instead of reinforcing the first one? It's simple, isn't it? **Because it's the only thing society can do.** Think about it, even if society wants to punish me, it can't. How can it?

What's the point of the rules, really?

I'm sure you're wondering then,

*"But then, **why** did society come up with rules at all? What purpose do they serve?"*

The purpose is simple. These rules were created by people like me to reduce competition for ourselves. That's what I said about holding yourself to a higher calling than everyone else!

Alright, I'm sure you're asking then, *"Wow, Professor. So you're telling me there's like a secret society of 'people like you,' who make up rules to control others... but don't enforce the rules, so they themselves can break them without consequences? What is this society, and can I join?"*

And the answer is, of course you can join! You just start becoming honest with yourself and start living free!

"But how, Professor?" you ask. *"I could never be as honest and free as someone amazing like you. Don't you just have to be born a sociopath? Obviously, it's a compliment. I mean, I wish I was a sociopath. That'd solve all my problems!"*

But no, dear Reader, that's a myth. I've met them all, and nobody's born like that. Maybe for some women it's more innate. Some women can do things without thinking, and later justify their actions with their feelings. That's women's superpower. Ironically, they often have bigger balls than most men! But not all women are like that. There are plenty of women who are constantly anxious about everything.

And certainly, most men aren't like that at all. Men are too logical, they need things to "make sense." That's fine, it just means we need to build everything up.

You see, I wasn't born this way, although it was always inevitable for me. I still remember that in my childhood, I spent a lot of time crying at the stupidity of people. Then I spent just as much time laughing at the stupidity of people. Then I was laughing and crying at the same time.

I mean, just think about it. What's with all these people following non-existing rules? Even when I was a toddler, I always fought tooth and nail when someone dared tell me what to do. But why is no one else fighting?

It took me a very long time to realize it, but let me just tell you straight up. It's obvious, isn't it? **Because people are Homer Simpsons. And Homers love rules!**

What are rules, really?

In essence, rules are answers to life. For example, say you become a Catholic and give up meat on Fridays. Well, at first you'd be upset. It'd take you a while to go through the five stages of grief. But a few weeks later, you'd accept it. And now, you're happier than before! Because you now have the answer to one more question in life: "What to eat on Friday?" And you never need to worry about it again. And the more answers you have, the happier you are!

So don't feel guilty about imposing rules on others. Don't worry about telling them what to do. You're doing them a favor! Because they want to be told how to live their lives. The average man absolutely needs permission before he can do anything, otherwise, he will do nothing! And after he does something, don't forget to compliment him and validate him, otherwise, he'll never do it again!

"But if you give them too many unfair rules, that can backfire, right? Because they'll fight back?"

Hahahaha, that's the fun part. They need to be told how to fight back too! So you just need to tell them to only fight within the rules you established!

***

My student Andrew told me a while back about an author called Orwell. Apparently, he wrote some **very dangerous books** that expose how totalitarian governments control people. For example, it's said governments worldwide are afraid of his 1984 book because of how accurate it is.

Wow, what a dangerous book… I guess such a book must be banned, right?

No… wait a minute, it's not banned anywhere. It's never even banned in Russia or China. And actually, here in the West, **they're taught at schools!**

But hold on. Do you see a problem? If these books are so dangerously accurate, if governments are so afraid of these books… why would they teach them at school? It's almost like they want you to read them!

Well, what do you think? Of course they want you to read it. Because they want to say, "Look at these **cartoonishly evil governments**, this is how totalitarian governments work. But we're not as cartoonishly evil as them. Which means we're not totalitarian and you're not being controlled!"

Just look around you. Do the government need to put surveillance everywhere? Or are people gladly volunteering their location, their data, showcasing every moment of their life?

Do the media feed you blatantly contradictory statements? Or is everyone getting echo chambers on social media? Even AI is busy agreeing with you all the time.

Most importantly, are most people driven by fear? Or are they driven by **comfort**?

These days in London, you can't go a few days without hearing people complain. "The knife gangs are taking over the streets! People are getting stabbed everywhere! The grooming gangs need to be stopped! I've had enough of this!"

Well, what are you going to do about it?

"I'm going to go on **protests**, and I'm going to **vote out the current leadership.**"

Hahahahaha! Vote them out? When? In the next General Election in four years? What if they rig the elections?

You quickly find that most people don't have a good answer to this. Because most of them believe, deep down, that elections are real. Why? Is there transparency? Is there accountability? Do you understand every step of the system? No. But people still believe in it. Why?

Because it's a comfortable thought! Isn't election great? You don't need to actually fight back and risk getting hurt. You don't need to go out there and defend your children. You don't need to do any hard work or make any sacrifices. You can just sit in your comfort chair, in the comfort of your own home, and still change the world! By voting! Zero effort, maximum rewards!

Listen, there are a couple of countries in the world where their history is just an endless series of civil wars, rebellions, revolutions, and uprisings. People start rebellions for the most ridiculous reason, and tens of millions of people die each time. They have no illusion of "democracy" either, so they take matters into their own hands and start waging wars. There, the governments are actually afraid of their people, which is why they put surveillance everywhere and keep a tight control of the population.

But here in the English-speaking world? Has uprisings like that ever happened? People are conditioned for generations to obey. You can poke them, provoke them, impose rules on them, and what do they do? They vote! They're playing by the system's rules, while convinced they're "fighting back"! It's like when they read a government-endorsed book, and are convinced they're being a rebel.

Now, readers might have one of two reactions up to this point. Some might feel offended or **uncomfortable**, some might think I'm being cynical or negative, and hope I talk about something happier and more **comfortable** instead. Whatever.

Some people are depressed. *"I hate that people are Homer Simpsons! How do we change them? How do we wake the people up? How do we make the world a better place?"*

Hahaha, what? Wake the people up? Make the world a better place? Are you stupid?

Now, a few of you, however, might feel excited and liberated. *"Rules don't exist? I can break any rule I want? And people are just that passive that they don't even fight back? Sounds like it's easy to win! Tell me more!* ***How do I win?****"*

Exactly! That's the right question to ask! And this is exactly the right book for you!

You've been conditioned your entire life for comfort, so the first step is to destroy the comfortable lies. It takes courage, but it's worth it. And there's nothing more worthwhile, because you're going to finally experience true liberation!

And maybe you still want to change the world, too? Yeah, my postdoc Alison is like that, always talking about "justice" or "finding the best outcome for everyone." Ugh. She's still learning from me, not because she realized how naïve she was, but because she wants to "learn enough so she can defeat me one day." The arrogance!

Well, I'll tell you what I told her: if you want to go up against people like me, **you can't be stupid.** You need to become more vicious than me. So stick around if you want. It's up to you whatever you want to do with the knowledge. Either way, let's move on!

3

NO SUCH THING AS SELF-DOUBT, ONLY HYPOCRISY

You can't go anywhere in life if you doubt yourself. So we're going to destroy your self-doubt first. In any case, it's very easy.

The truth is you cannot doubt yourself without being a hypocrite. All your unhappiness, anxiety, depression, self-doubt, insecurity… everything comes down to one thing: **hypocrisy!**

You already saw hypocritical rules in the previous chapter, but hypocrisy comes in so many other forms too. What have you been told all your life since the day you went to school? You were told to:

- *"Be brave and speak the truth,"* but also, *"If it's not nice, don't say it!"*

- So should I speak the truth, or should I not say it then? Which one is it?

- *"Be yourself," but also, "Be likable and make friends!"*

  - So should I be myself, or should I be likable, meaning appeasing others? Should I try to do both at the same time? But shouldn't you have focus and priorities? Shouldn't you have clear principles and values?

- *"Critical thinking," but also, "Trust the experts!"*

- *"Everyone is equal," but also, "Check your privilege!"*

- *"Take risks," but also, "Don't offend!"*

- *"Follow your heart," but also, "Follow what's right!"*

- *"Don't burn bridges," but also, "Stand up for your principles, no matter the cost!"*

- *"Money can't buy happiness" and "money is the root of all evil," implying wanting money is bad. But also, "People commit crimes not because they're bad, but because poverty and inequality push them to it."*

  - So wanting money leads to evil, but not having money pushes me to crimes? Should I want money or not want money then?

- *"Be humble and open-minded," but also, "Have strong boundaries and stand up for your beliefs."*

  - Boundaries cannot be open by definition. It's basic topology!

Or there are "feel-good" lies that everyone parrots, but you know deep down to be false.

- *"Work hard, be kind, and amazing things will happen to you."* You might as well believe in "Do good, and you'll be rewarded in the afterlife." Sounds like the same thing to me!

- *"Treat others like you want to be treated."* Are you going to babysit the entire world? It's not up to you to enforce other people's boundaries.

- *"If you want to lift yourself up, lift up someone else."* Is this how Corporate America works? Has this worked out well for you?

Some people might object to some of these, "You can have strong boundaries and open minds at the same time, here is how…"

And this is followed by 10 minutes of mental gymnastics and rhetorical jujitsu. Listen, you're making life complicated for yourself. You can spend years sorting out every little nuance, which your subconscious mind wouldn't understand anyway. Or you can follow Einstein's advice, "if you can't explain it to a 6-year-old, you don't understand it enough." Which is true! Life isn't complicated, it's only complicated if you're stupid, so don't be stupid! Smart people always simplify!

Anything in "self-help" and psychology is full of traps

For every guru that tells you to "set S.M.A.R.T. goals," another says "be process-driven, not outcome-driven." Often the same person says both things. Well, which is it?

It's also the case in a lot of sciences. You know how it goes. For every research paper that says drinking coffee or a glass of wine is bad for you, another says it's good for you. For every research that says chocolate causes cancer, another says it helps prevent cancer. And this is still real science.

What about "social" science, like the unfalsifiable pseudoscience of psychology? It's so much worse!

- For every psychologist who says "venting and letting it all out" is good, another says "practicing an emotion produces a feedback loop", in other words, letting out your anger makes you more angry.

- For every research that says high self-esteem prevents anything bad, another says it leads to narcissism.

- One moment, Cognitive Behavioral Therapy is good, the next moment, it's only superficial symptom management.

Some say, *"But this is how science works. Science is not a straight line, new theories replace old theories…"*

No, this is not how science works… this is how pseudoscience pretending to be science works! Because there is never any "replacing" in social sciences. They never retract old theories. They just let contradictory theories flood the Internet!

***

Having these contradictions is like telling a computer to go left and right at the same time. It's going to be confused, and it's going to freeze. If you have any self-doubt, anxiety, shame… anything at all, it means somewhere deep within you, there is some hypocrisy.

Think about it, someone living a perfectly coherent life, with a perfectly coherent worldview, who always knows what to do in each situation, who has the answers to all the questions… will not have reasons to doubt themselves. Any doubts come from some sort of incoherence.

Some traps are very insidious

Often you get trapped just by engaging in a discussion, just by accepting the premise. Take the word "homophobia", that's them putting words into your mouth, by saying you have "fear." What a bigoted idea! This word has no place in modern society. Because why would anyone be afraid of homosexuals?

Well, the only reason you'd be afraid of them, it would be that you're afraid of being sexually assaulted by him. But that's just a negative stereotype from prison and military! It's not true anywhere else!

So, just by using the word "homophobia," you're implying homosexuals are sexual offenders! How homophobic!

That's why the modern and correct term should be "homoloathic," because most people don't feel fear, they feel queasy and grossed out.

And they call homophobia a "hate speech." Again, they're putting words into your mouth. There are people who argue that "Hate speech is free speech!" But that's a trap, and they already lost the battle just by using the phrase. It should be either "fear speech" or "disgust speech".

It sounds like a lot of these were invented by the progressives to trap the conservatives, doesn't it? Is there a global conspiracy going on? Well, not really. Truth is, the progressives trap themselves more than they trap others!

I heard just the other day that some progressive folks unironically speak against "slut-shaming." Like "we should stop slut-shaming." Isn't that just the sort of stupidity that makes you want to laugh and cry at the same time?

If they want to defend promiscuity, why call it "shaming"? If they want to be proud of being sluts, why not call it "slut-honoring"? Maybe that's too ridiculous even for them? But the moment they called it "shaming," they already lost the battle. These people think they're fighting for freedom? They're trapped at a fundamental level!

When a female athlete thinks she's inspiring a group of girls, saying "If you work hard and persevere, **you too can beat the guys!**" She thinks she's empowering, but really she's humiliating, because she's implying women aren't already better than the guys. Why not? Women are more intuitive, more emotionally mature, they're better socially, so why aren't women better already? Why do they have to compete in things involving strength and violence? Because she thinks deep down masculine qualities are superior to feminine qualities, and she's spreading her inferiority to others!

Same with the debates on gendered toys. Activists funded by toy stores want girls to play boys' toys. Like "girls should ditch the dolls and start building Lego bridges."

Huh? Why do you want your daughter to build bridges? Do you want her to become an engineer? But engineering is just low-level physics, why would you want her to work in something so stupid? Isn't playing with dolls infinitely better than building bridges in every sense?

Anyway, that's what introduced hypocrisy and contradictions to a lot of women's minds, and why the progressive people are all depressed. You know, I heard people comparing the progressive movement at university to a cult. Well, you're giving them too much credit. It's the worst cult ever! The point of a cult is to make money, but the progressive movement is a money-sink. That's why it's a dying movement that's doomed to fail.

But it's not hopeless. If I were to consult for them, I can easily revive the transgender movement and keep people distracted from the class war even after AI. Tell Soros I'm ready.

How to liberate yourself from traps

Now you see these traps are everywhere! And they can be very insidious. And if you don't feel 100% in control of your life, something must be trapping you.

By the way, this is why religious people are much happier. Because they have an ultimate authority figure telling them exactly what to do in which situation, and it's not up for debate. If they ever get confused, they can always open up the Bible or talk to a pastor and get a definitive answer, no thinking required!

That's why for most people, religion is a great choice! After all, if you don't believe in God, you'll have to believe in humans. But humans are imperfect. Everything man-made is full of contradictions and hypocrisy. That's why people are unhappy these days.

In that case, you must be very suspicious of any and every outside influence. First of all, you need to have very strong boundaries. That means you should not have an open mind.

Open mind is stupid. Having an open mind is like leaving your house unlocked and windows wide open, hoping that some genius accidentally wanders in and gives you some wisdom. But what are the odds? The majority of the time, you're going to get idiots come in to scribble nonsense on the wall.

I, for example, do not have open minds. I have constructed an impenetrable fortress against all my enemies—stupidity, hypocrisy, psychology, the French. If someone wants to so much as take a peek into my mind, they'll have to pay for it. That's why this book isn't free.

And by the way, that's also why I don't read feedback, so don't waste your energy writing to me. If you have questions, you can send one question per book purchase to professor@raymondmarylowe.com. Attach a selfie of you holding this book, so my VA will forward it to me and I will reply. But don't send us opinions, I don't read opinions. I don't look up my name on the Internet, I don't read book reviews. If I ever want feedback I'd ask someone actually qualified. And here's the thing about people who are actually qualified—they never give advice for free!

Anyway, here's something else to help you see through the traps: **simplify**. Simplify everything, start with your language. Follow Einstein's advice: talk to everyone like they're six years old. Simple words are weapons, used by people who play to win. They let you see the world for what it really is.

Big words are fogs to hide behind, used by people who play to not lose. But then those fogs end up trapping them, confusing them, and paralyzing them. That's why pretentious pseudo-intellectuals all have depression, see? They think they're having deep thoughts, but really it's mental noise. Truly smart people know the world is very simple to understand, because we've already figured it out!

Reject all psychological labels

Other than non-existent rules and contradictory nonsense, the only weapon society has is psychological labels. That's why these labels are always defective, and always there to pathologize.

Being active is a good thing. In this day and age, it's practically a superpower! So why did they call it "hyperactivity disorder"? Why not "hyperactivity superiority"?

Why did they call it "autistic spectrum disorder"? Why not "autistic spectrum advantage"? Autistic people who don't care about social rules have as many advantages as they have supposed "disadvantages!"

There are these psychologists who tell you to celebrate and embrace your labels. Sounds great—except these labels are literally always called disorders! Where are the labels that describe how amazing you are? They don't exist! All of the labels are only designed to pathologize you, to limit you, to put you in a trap, telling you you're defective and inferior! That includes even the "good" labels like IQ.

The tale of Mensa society—a society of morons...

In case you don't know, Mensa society is a society where you need a very high IQ to join. You need an IQ of 130 or so, or top 2%. It's said to be a society of geniuses... of intellectuals...

Hahaha... Don't make my face laugh. It's a society of morons!

Let's think about what this means. If you judge someone's intelligence, it means you have to be smarter than them. Are you following me?

Because if someone is more stupid than me, how can they judge my intelligence? They can't even comprehend what's going on in my mind!

So if you let someone judge your intelligence, you've accepted you're more stupid than them.

But these people in the Mensa society let **social scientists** judge their intelligence by labeling them with IQ scores? What does it say? It says **they're more stupid than social scientists!**

But if you're more stupid than social scientists... what does that say about you? You're mentally retarded! I'm sorry!

(By the way, I don't mean "I apologize," I meant I'm sorry that you folks at Mensa society are mentally retarded.)

Listen, humans are flawed, so humans can't judge. God alone can judge. And if you let psychologists judge you, then who becomes your God now? If you have to accept someone as your God, might as well choose Jesus Christ, at least he's said to love you and have your best interest in mind. Can social scientists say the same?

The reality is, if the morons in Mensa society were smarter, they'd know **psychology is an unfalsifiable pseudo-science and IQ is all made up!** Read on.

4

Psychology Is An Unfalsifiable Pseudo-Science

Psychological labels are the final weapon society uses to make you conform. Things like "narcissist," "psychopath," "sociopath," or maybe "depression," "imposter syndrome," "autistic," "ADHD," "low IQ."

Most people are trapped by them one way or another. But not me. And you know why? Because I know psychology is an unfalsifiable pseudo-science, and psychologists are all science-deniers! Let me free you from this pseudo-scientific nonsense.

1. Clinical psychology is not falsifiable

Read this conversation between a psychologist and his patient.

* * *

Psychologist: "It's become quite clear to me. You fall within the spectrum of **Narcissistic Personality Disorder**."

Patient: "Huh? That can't be true… Aren't narcissists supposed to be self-centered? But I have meaningful friendships, I spend time with my friends and I worry about their well-being. I'm not selfish."

Psychologist: "Yes, but that's the textbook definition of a **high-functioning narcissist**. You find these friendships meaningful because they validate your self-image as a 'good friend'. These people are not individuals to you, they're sources of narcissistic supply. You say you 'worry' about them, but it's simply a defense mechanism to ensure that supply chain remains stable."

Patient: "What!? Okay, but… I also have self-doubt. I constantly question myself. I thought narcissists were supposed to be pathologically over-confident."

Psychologist: "Ah, but that's a classic case of **covert narcissism**, where you use outward display of self-doubt to elicit pity and reassurance from others. Instead of demanding admiration directly, you manipulate others into offering it freely out of sympathy. Truly a highly sophisticated tactic!"

Patient: "This is absurd! I'm sure normal people do these things too! It's not like I do it more than anyone else, you can't call it a disorder!"

Psychologist: "Instead of meaningful self-reflection, look how quickly you dismiss the possibility. This is the very definition of **denial and emotional repression**, a refusal to confront the underlying pathology."

Patient: "Yeah!? This is ridiculous! I—I reject your diagnosis. I think it's a load of crap!"

Psychologist: "And there you have it. The final, definitive marker: **narcissistic rage**. An extreme, aggressive, and disproportionate reaction to having your fragile ego challenged by a professional diagnosis. Thank you for this textbook demonstration. Our session is complete."

Patient: "What?!"

* * *

Do you see the problem here, smart reader? No matter what you say, they can twist it to support their diagnosis. You can't prove them wrong! This is the textbook demonstration of **unfalsifiable, pseudo-scientific nonsense.** By definition:

- A science is something falsifiable, "It can be proven or disproven by experiments."

- A pseudo-science is something unfalsifiable, "It can't be proven or disproven by experiments."

And psychology is by definition unfalsifiable, therefore it's a pseudo-science. This is not an opinion, it's a fact. It's based on black and white logic. No amount of argument or social science research can change this. Logic is irrefutable.

For example, take the idea that "IQ is related to intelligence." Can it be proven or disproven by experiment? No. Because we don't know how to measure intelligence. That's why they invented IQ. But is IQ a good measure? No one knows!

What about "arrogance is a sign of narcissism"? Again unfalsifiable. How are you going to prove it or disprove it? You can't! It's equivalent to saying "confidence is a trait of

Leo." And yes, psychology is exactly like astrology, both are unfalsifiable pseudo-sciences.

"But everyone says psychology is legit, so it must be! Most scientists think IQ is a good measure, so it must be! Psychology is also very useful! It also has more funding than astrology, it's researched at university!"

So what? Science is not democracy. Science is not defined by funding. Science is not about "usefulness." Science doesn't care about your feelings. Science is about **falsifiability**.

Is psychology useful? I have no doubt! It's certainly interesting. And it's useful precisely because it's interesting! **But it's not science.**

You object. *"But there are fields like behavioral psychology—they **are** falsifiable, right?"*

Ah yes, they're better, they're also not the ones trying to pathologize you. Still, take their research with a grain of salt. If you think they can give you easy answers to life, you'd be very disappointed. Because most psychological research is wrong! And that brings us to...

2. Psychology is not reproducible

More than 50% of psychology research is not reproducible. This is the so-called "reproducibility crisis." More than 50%! You'd be better off flipping coins!

By the way, have they done anything to fix the issue? To put out the fire? The only thing they did was to start the "open science" movement about 10 years ago. It means researchers now have to publish their **raw data**, not just the conclusion.

But think about what this means... for more than a century, they never needed to publish raw data? They only invented transparency 10 years ago?!

That's right. Truth is, even if you publish raw data, it means nothing, because raw data can be made up or manipulated. But for 140 years, their so-called "research" didn't even need raw data, it was literally just "trust me, I'm a scientist!" Now you see why more than 50% can't be reproduced!

Anyway, to fix the crisis, the only way would be to lower error rates. That includes false-positives (p-value), and false-negatives (power). Has these been changed?

No, **neither has been changed.** Ask AI if you don't believe me.

Worst part is... they never retracted any papers! They only retracted some downright fraudulent research. The majority of the wrong research is still online!

When a research couldn't be reproduced in physics, like cold fusion, pentaquarks, faster-than-light neutrinos... whether it's honest error or downright fraud, the original paper was retracted and destroyed. Often, the researcher's career is over! Purged! Their reputation is ruined!

But in psychology? There's no consequence at all! And these wrong research continues to be read, cited, and used to create more theories! The whole of psychology is built on a rotten foundation.

3. Data can be easily manipulated

There is a famous paper "Same Data, Different Conclusions" which demonstrates this. When different researchers interpret the same data, they reach drastically different conclusions, as much as 300% differences!

4. Clinical psychology is all about self-reporting

Before science, all knowledge was self-reporting. "I feel this herb cures me," "I believe this planet brings me good luck." But then we figured out it's a bad idea to trust people, because people are unreliable idiots! They're not trustworthy and they lie! That's why we have the scientific method. We have measurement, replication, falsification, all created to remove self-reporting.

But what is clinical psychology? It's **fundamentally all self-reporting.** "I feel depressed," "I feel happier after taking this pill," "On a scale of 1-10 I feel like a 7." It launched society right back to the middle ages.

5. Statistics cannot describe individuals

Psychology Is An Unfalsifiable Pseudo-Science

This is a screenshot I took from the NYTimes website. It's a news article right before the 2016 election, and it read: "The New York Times Presidential Forecast, Tuesday, October 18, 2016, Hillary Clinton has a 91% chance to win."

First of all, hilarious prediction, right? Because Trump won. But that's not the issue here. Let's focus on the "91% chance to win." What does it mean? No, think about it. What's the meaning of 91%?

Does it mean she wins 91% of the time? No, because there is only one election.

Does it mean in 100 parallel universes, she will win in 91 of them? Maybe. But we don't live in a parallel universe, so it doesn't matter!

What's the point of the 91%? Well, it's meaningless, **it doesn't mean anything!** It's a misuse of statistics!

It's like when a doctor tells you, "You have cancer, your 5-year survival rate is 60%."

What does the "60%" mean? It means nothing! It might mean something to the doctor who has to manage a bunch of patients. But for you as an individual? The number "60%" is meaningless! **Because you either die or you won't die.** Statistics can't describe one-off events!

During WWII, there was a psychologist who did a "psycho-analysis" on Hitler, and concluded Hitler had a very **high chance** of committing suicide. And when Hitler did commit suicide, the psychologist looked like a genius...

... but what does "high chance" mean? **Hitler either commits suicide, or he doesn't commit suicide.** Again, it's meaningless. It's not science, it's pseudo-science using the language of statistics to mimic real science.

That's why all diagnosis in clinical psychology is meaningless. For example, when they say "you have a **high risk of relapsing**"—it means nothing. And when they diagnose mental illnesses? Their tests are subjective, they can't be 100% accurate. So really, it means "There is a chance you're a narcissist/psychopath/sociopath…"

But these statements are all fundamentally meaningless, because chances don't apply to individuals!

* * *

But that's not all, there is more! Are you ready for me to drop the nuclear bomb? Are you ready for me to annihilate their field altogether?

6. Mental illnesses do not exist by definition

When they diagnose mental illnesses, do they use a brain scan? No. They use questionnaires and interviews. Because none of the illnesses can be detected!

You might say, *"But depression is definitely real, because I* ***feel*** *it. And if we haven't found it yet, that just means we need to invent better scanners!"*

Ah, yes. But even if one day they do find depression, or autism, or ADHD in the brain… **then it'd no longer be a mental illness… it'd become a brain disease!** And it'd be treated by real doctors like neurologists and brain surgeons, not fake doctors like psychologists. So mental illnesses don't exist and cannot exist, by definition!

Well, society has truly regressed. At least with religion, we don't know if God exists. But with psychology, you're dealing with things that don't exist by definition!

***

A lot of people throw psychology labels around like insults. Things like "sociopath" or "narcissist." But you're trapping nobody but yourself!

- You accuse people of being sociopaths... but real sociopaths don't care about your opinion.

- You accuse people of being psychopaths... but real psychopaths don't care about your opinion.

- You accuse people of being a narcissist... but real narcissists are now happier because they just got attention from you.

You achieve nothing, except now you're trapped! Because you just accepted these labels are real, and they're "bad." Now you're going through life being extra careful, "Am I being a narcissist?" "Is this sociopathic behavior?" You'll never win with this sort of self-doubt and hesitation!

When you try to shame people to conform, you're shaming nobody but yourself. The only response is to see psychology for what it really is: an unfalsifiable pseudo-science, and reject it outright.

Science has nothing to do with "truth"

A lot of people have the wrong idea about science. They think it's a scientist's job to find truth. That's wrong! Do you know any truth? I've been a theoretical physicist my entire life and I don't know a single truth. The reality is in science we don't have truth, we have **models**. All models are wrong, but some are useful. Like the Homer Simpson model is extremely useful. And a scientist's job isn't to find truth, but to **find evidence**.

When social scientists claims to have "truth", what they really have is an **agenda**. Truth does not come from science. Truth comes from **logic**. For example, "psychology is unfalsifiable, therefore it's pseudo-science." This is logic. It's a deeper truth than any psychological research. No amount of "research," opinion, consensus, or backlash can change the logical fact.

* * *

I hear you saying: *"Everything you said makes perfect sense, Professor. But wait a minute, if scientists can twist statistics to get whatever conclusion they want, how do I know what **you** said is true? How do I know I can trust **you**?"*

Hahaha, what do you think? I guess there is no way for you to know! That's the whole point! The only way to make sure you're **not** being manipulated by me is to get better at statistics manipulation than me. But that'd take you years, and you don't need to. It just comes down to one simple thing:

Reject. You already know to reject popular opinion and societal rules. Now you know to reject psychology. Reject social science. Reject their "research." It's all one lie on top of another. They might look respectable with their suits or their big beards, but see them for what they really are: all social scientists are monkeys and downright frauds. If they tell you something is true, it's false. If they tell you to do something, do the opposite.

5

God Alone Can Judge

"*Professor, so **everything** is a lie? **Nothing** is real? Nobody can be trusted?*"

I know, amazing, right? Now while the rest of the miserable people get trapped by non-existent rules, doubt themselves, are constantly paralyzed, or addicted to drugs, you're now free!

"*But I feel lost! I feel I'm in a vacuum with nothing to hold onto! Please, can you stop tearing things down, but instead start **telling us what to believe in?** Can you **tell us what to do?***"

Hahaha! Listen, vacuum is a great place to be in because there is no resistance. Besides, you're not nearly in a vacuum yet.

Even people who see through fake social rules still obey them, because they fear social judgment. This is the final piece of the puzzle you must eliminate. But why do people fear judgment? Only because they're judging others.

- If you judge others, you will necessarily worry about being judged by others.
- If you don't judge others, you will automatically stop worrying about judgments from others.

So you should stop judging. Not only because it serves you, but also because judging is stupid.

Erase the lies of "divine punishment" or "karmic justice"

Let's talk about God for a second. When bad things happen to them, people ask, "Why did God let this happen?"

It's a degree of narcissistic, self-righteous, delusional entitlement even I cannot fathom! Do you think that's what God is, some cosmic police officer? He has nothing better to do than running after us humans, cleaning up **your** mess, righting wrongs for **you**?

You see injustice in the world? Then go fight it! Didn't God already give you "free will" and a perfectly capable body? What else do you need? If you really want to achieve something, there is always a way.

But obviously, fighting injustice is too much work, too much risk. If only you could just say some prayers, and God would come take care of things for you. That'd be much easier! Well, say your prayers all day long if you want. But you see, there is no evidence the world operates on thoughts, feelings, and prayers. The world operates on actions and initiatives.

Some say, "You shouldn't murder, because God will punish you for it." Others say "All these atrocities are proof that God doesn't exist!"

You're confusing the marketing for the product. Here's where God comes into this: the average person is lazy and terrified, very few are capable of murder. That's why throughout history, they need God to make themselves feel righteous and be decisive. The "evil" people commit atrocities precisely because they believed they had goodness on their side.

There are even people who say "the West is falling because it abandoned God." If that's the case, Godless countries like China must be failing. Wait a minute, it's not failing, it's overtaking the West! How come?!

It's simple cause and effect. The average person needs to be told what to do, otherwise they will do nothing. And in China, the Party is the ultimate authority telling everyone what to do. There is no debate, there is total coherence.

In the West, we replaced God with a thousand smaller but weaker ones. We instead have pseudo-scientists and political activists with their self-contradicting ideologies. So the average person doesn't even know what to believe in anymore. Result: paralysis for everyone!

Erase the lies of "deserving" and "fairness"

My friend **the Senator, an elite criminal lawyer** once said,

"You don't get what you deserve, you get what you fight for."

And he's absolutely right. Words like "expectations" or "high standards" or "deserving" don't have any meaning. If you think you deserve something, go fight for it! Otherwise, it's called being lazy and entitled.

What about fairness? Someone complained to me once, about this famous blind magician who went on becoming rich and famous. But in reality, this magician wasn't even blind. He faked his blindness to get sympathy and popularity. He even stole from other magicians' magic tricks!

"Do you think that's fair?" The man asked me. "That while real artists are struggling, a fraud like him ended up becoming rich and famous?"

Huh? But what exactly is unfair about it? He sounds exactly like the kind of person who would become rich and famous!

The world doesn't run on feelings. The world runs on cause and effect. When people say "this is not fair," really they mean "I don't understand how this works." So here's something to help you understand how things work: remember correlations always imply causation! You just need to look hard enough.

- Why do these "good" people get scammed? Maybe precisely because they're "good"! Scammers don't target other scammers!

- Why do "evil" people succeed in life? Why shouldn't they? And maybe you're not a very good judge of character, and you should let God alone judge good and evil.

- Why aren't "evil-doers" punished? Maybe because everybody's too busy asking stupid questions like this, and nobody is actually out there punishing them!

Erase the lies of "integrity" and "dignity"

What is integrity? Integrity means completeness and wholeness. It means total coherence, free from contradictions and hypocrisy. Integrity is often lumped with honesty. But that can't be true! Because what does honesty mean? Is it being honest to myself, or being honest to others?

Say you're applying for a job, the hiring manager asks you, "Please answer honestly, what is your biggest weakness?"

Well, if you're truly honest, you'd say, "If I'm being honest, I think you're a creep and you don't deserve to know the truth!"

Hahaha, yes! So lie to him to get the job! That's called being true to your goals, that's what true integrity is about!

Some people say "lying is bad" or "lying is not a long-term strategy." Says who? You just need to get better. Abraham Lincoln once said, "You can fool some of the people all of the time, you can fool all of the people some of the time, but you can't fool Mom." But when you get to the highest level—the level I'm at—I can even fool my Mom!

What about dignity? But why do you want it? It's so boring! The equation of life isn't complicated:

- If you focus on chasing money... you'll get money!

- If you focus on chasing girls... you'll get girls!

- If you focus on chasing dignity... you'll get dignity!

But what can you do with dignity? You can't do anything with it!

Some people think, "But dignity is useful if you want respect! I can't be seen beg or cry or embarrass myself or show vulnerability. Then people lose respect of me!"

Your first issue is you want respect. That means you're still seeing other people as your equal. Not to mention vulnerability has nothing to do with respect. You just need to get better. It reminds me of this reader who wrote to me, with full admiration,

"Professor... my girlfriend said she liked it when guys show vulnerability. So one night, I opened up and poured my heart out to her, I got emotional, and I even cried and wept a bit... she consoled me then. But now, she said she lost all attraction to me after seeing me cry! And she broke up with me! That's when I realized, the so-called 'vulnerability' is a lie!

"But... when I read your story in The Physicist Detective, in that scene where Matilda found out you were chatting up other women? You immediately dropped to your knees and started sobbing, pleading, weeping, full-on crying in her lap, begging for her forgiveness...

"And she forgave you? And ended up loving you even more? Can you tell me what happened? Why is it when you cried, things work out for you. But when I cried, my girlfriend left me?"

Hahahahaha! Because I'm amazing, that's why! Listen, your girlfriend didn't leave you because you cried, but because you're too boring. You just need to get better at it!

Erase the lie of "truth"

If there isn't even truth in theoretical physics... could there really be truth anywhere in the world? The answer is, no, of course not! There is no such thing as truth!

Only recently people start to realize I'm right. *"You know, Professor, you're right. With AI-generated videos and pictures, I even don't know what to trust anymore. Anything could be fake!"*

Of course. And you think AI changes anything, but really, AI changes nothing. Because before AI, there was photoshop. The Godfather warned all the way back in 1969 to not talk on the phone, as your voice could be spliced together to make you say anything. But even before that, there was fake news articles, fake eye witnesses. In fact, nothing has changed for hundreds of thousands of years. In the past, everything was hearsay, "he said, she said".

That's why the only thing you can trust is what you see with your own eye. In particular, you should not trust anything on the Internet, because **the Internet is not real.** That's why people on the Internet use the phrase "IRL"—meaning "in real life". That alone is proof enough that nothing on the Internet is real!

Some people say, "But the Internet seems pretty real to me!" As a matter of fact, I have on good authority the Internet is a conspiracy created by CERN to suppress their vulnerability in legacy structures. An old portable computer model IBM 5100 could read and debug any code in legacy mainstream systems, so CERN invented the WWW in 1989 to digitize all their valuable code, records, and systems into a modern format that the IBM 5100 couldn't access, so its abilities became obsolete, and corporate or governmental mainframe knowledge remains sealed. And so, let me repeat, nothing on the Internet is real! Even the Internet itself!

Erase the lies of "good" and "bad"

In the old days, philosophers were actually very smart. Because they know how to **simplify**. There's a Taoist story called "the old man lost his horse," I retell it here.

* * *

A man lived near the border. One day, his horse ran off into barbarian territory. The others in the village felt sorry for him. But the man said: "How do you know it's not a good thing?"

The next day, his horse came back, leading a group of barbarian horses. The others felt happy for him. But the man said: "How do you know it's not a bad thing?"

The man's son loved riding. The next day he tried to tame one of the barbarian horses, but fell and broke his leg. Everyone felt sorry for him. But the man said: "How do you know it's not a good thing?"

The next day, the barbarians invaded across the border, every able-bodied man was drafted into battles. Nine out of ten were killed. But the son was spared from the draft because of his injured legs.

* * *

Taoists created this Yin-Yang symbol to illustrate the point. There is good in bad, and there is bad in good. Good and bad aren't two opposite sides of a spectrum, they're intertwined with each other, in a cyclic motion. Something good can lead to bad, something bad can lead to good. **If there is one symbol that explains the whole world, this is it.**

Socrates was told by God he's the wisest man in the world, because he admits he knows nothing. "I know that I know nothing." He's right too.

The Bible also repeatedly said "Judge not, lest you be judged," and how God alone can judge, while humans cannot.

If you think about it: Taoism, Socrates, Bible... all three point to the same principle: humans are not God. We can never know the whole story, we cannot see into the past, we cannot predict the future, we cannot read minds. Our views are biased and our feelings are unreliable. Can we really judge? Of course not.

I always keep that in mind, which is why I never rush to conclusions and I never judge. In particular, I don't judge good or bad. I only judge people's stupidity. And now, you earned the right to judge others' stupidity too! What is stupidity?

A stupid person is someone who plays God, who thinks they can judge good from bad.

That's it! **Because it's impossible to know good from bad, period.** That's why psychologists are stupid, because they use words like "disorders." That's why wannabe-intellectuals like philosophers are stupid, because they use words like "moral" or "ethical." That's why social scientists are stupid, because they talk about things like "social justice."

You never see real scientists use language like this. Is gravity good or bad? It just is. Is a supernova good or bad? The question doesn't even make any sense. It is what it is.

If there's ever a "good" thing, it might be saving lives, which makes modern medicine the only definitive good thing in history. But even that is debatable. They say there's a real risk that superbugs might launch us back to the pre-antibiotic era yet. We simply don't know!

"Good" and "bad" depends on perspectives

The British Empire was having 6-year-olds working in coal mines, women were exploited in textile factories—very "bad," right? If we lived in a "fair" world, such an Empire would surely have gotten "divine punishment."

Well, the punishment certainly didn't come in their lifetime, because it became the largest empire in history! Of course it would. It had more people working in factories than every other country, how could it not dominate world trade? And this improved the standard of living for everyone. How could you say it's not a good thing?

But then again, who says it's not a bad thing? We're seeing the effects now. People got lazy and entitled, they asked for too much pay and too many rights. They refuse to be exploited. So now the government human traffics boatloads of illegal immigrants to exploit them instead. And now the native British are complaining about losing their jobs and the gang violence on the street.

But then again, who says it's not a good thing? On the one side, you have gangs who operate on force and violence. On the other side, you have the native British, apparently their jobs are being taken away, their countrymen are getting stabbed, their children are being groomed, the streets of London red with blood. And what are they doing in response? Nothing! They go on a protest here and there, believing in the politicians to solve their problems for them!

Tell me, which group is more "deserving" of winning? Would it be "fair" for these deluded people to get what they want? Which group would God "favor" more?

Anyway, I'm ready for the Islamic takeover. Hopefully under Sharia law they'd void my prenup, and I'd be allowed to have multiple wives too. Matilda can't even say no to me!

"Good" and "bad" change depending on where you are

For example, you think being "narcissistic" is bad. But if you just go to any Third World country, which is 80% of the world, every single one of us Westerners would be diagnosed as a narcissist!

With our social media use? Constantly broadcasting our private lives? Setting "personal goals" instead of "family goals"? "Finding yourself"? "Self-fulfillment"? "Self-care"? Pursuit of individual happiness over collective well-being? How many people are preaching "community-first" or "tribe-first"? No. They teach you "Don't compromise what you want for anyone." Oh my God, textbook narcissist!

What about when you scroll past images of wars, famines, and natural disasters in other countries? You shake your head and sigh. You feel a flicker of sadness, just enough to react with a "love" or "care" emoji. And you go back to scrolling. How could you be so callous? Can't you at least pretend to care more? What a sociopath!

But you see, that's why words like "narcissist" or "sociopath" are meaningless. Otherwise, you, me, everyone you know in the Western world, we'd all be clinically and pathologically diagnosed with narcissism and sociopathy by 80% of the world!

But more importantly, how do you know that's not a good thing? Maybe the West is successful precisely because we're so narcissistic and sociopathic! If we're less narcissistic, why would we use social media at all? And if we stop showing off all our stuff on social media, why would we buy anything? We'd have a national GDP of 0 dollars!

And I can tell you, narcissism is a good thing for you too!

Listen, if there is anything definitively "bad" for you, it'd be **complaining**. It literally does nothing good at all! It's the most useless thing you could do, and I suggest you spend 0 seconds of your life complaining.

But if there is anything definitively "good," it would be **gratitude**. Everyone agrees it makes you happier. There are zero downsides. That's why everyone tells you to "practice gratitude."

But nobody knows how to. They repeat affirmations to themselves, saying "I'm thankful." But that just sounds hollow and doesn't work.

Here's how you actually practice gratitude: you need to see how things can benefit you. Then you're automatically grateful! That's how you feel genuine appreciation.

And what is narcissism? **Narcissism is hyper-gratitude.** It's the ability to look at anything and see how it benefits you personally. That's why "narcissists" are all very happy. Because they go through life appreciative of everything, they're forever grateful and literally cannot be unhappy!

"Good" and "bad" really means "natural" and "unnatural"

I remember this career summit me and my Inner Circle attended some time ago. A student asked me something like,

"So everything is made up. The system is broken, nothing in the world matters. Doesn't that mean everything is meaning-

less? You know there are two trillion galaxies in the universe, and we're just a speck of cosmic dust. What's the point, when nothing has meaning, and even success won't fill the void?"

What? What are you on about? People like to twist my words around. Who says nothing has meaning? In fact, everything has meaning. Here's what I'm actually saying: I'm telling you nothing is real, morality doesn't matter, and your actions have no consequences. I'm telling you this to help you become a winner! They're not excuses for being lazy losers!

Also, what even is "void"? I think these people listened to too many wannabe-intellectuals like philosophers and psychologists, now they're just imagining things that aren't there! They still don't understand the meaning of life? But it's so simple!

The meaning of life is survival and reproduction. If you're a man, you find meaning in improving your status. If you're a woman, in making your life more safe and secure. That's why, if there was any definition of "good" and "bad" at all, it's really "natural" and "unnatural." What is natural is by definition good, and what is unnatural is by definition not good. This is an undeniable fact in the universe.

I explained it to the student but he wasn't happy. *"That's it?! But survival for what? Reproduction for what? Just to create new beings who suffer through more meaninglessness? Biology doesn't explain human fulfillment! Where's the nobility in a life reduced to just machinery!?"*

But who says there isn't nobility? In fact, hold that thought, because if you want to see true nobility, I have a video of a dog I can show all of you later. It's so good, it's going to blow your mind.

But if nothing is real, what can we believe in?

Both of my students, Alison and Andrew, asked me that question at some point. "What can we believe in?" There are only a few answers to that question. I don't think you're ready for my answer yet. It's so powerful that your brain would melt. So let me first pass the pen to my friend, the Senator, and let him give his answer.

If you read my previous book, *The Physicist Detective vs. the Criminal Defense Lawyer*, you already know about him. He's a top-tier criminal lawyer from the States, but I guess he's what most people would call a "dirty lawyer," hahaha! We used to travel for a while, and let me tell you, he is a great young man to be around! He's slightly younger than me, though his hair is already completely silver, making him look like a superposition of a 20-year-old and a 60-year-old. He likes to talk about case studies instead of logic. But still, he's certainly one of the few people in the world with Big Brass Balls. You'd do well to pay close attention, because you'll learn a lot from him!

6

WHAT CAN YOU BELIEVE IN? (ACCORDING TO THE CRIMINAL DEFENSE LAWYER)

The Senator: So Professor Marylowe just broke you down, he exposed how everything in the world is fake, and you want to know what you can believe in. Allow me to give you my answer.

And did he just call me a "dirty lawyer"? Of course he was going to say that. But it's hardly fair, isn't it? Let me tell you my side of the story. Why don't I start with my first high-profile case? It's a class-action lawsuit, where I found myself on the side of the greedy corporate bully. This story will help answer all the questions you may have.

The Olympus Group case

I was a young associate, barely old enough to rent a car, working for one of the biggest firms in the country. My client in this case, I'll call it the Olympus Group for confidentiality, was a property development conglomerate.

Long story short, my client wanted to tear down a community hub and build a tower complex. It's the heart of the local community, with a free clinic, a subsidized daycare, a senior's meal program. Obviously, the locals weren't happy, and they filed a class-action lawsuit against us.

Their lead counsel was a respected veteran, but the real thorn in our side was his mentée, **Nicole**. She was a few years older than me. Brilliant, strong, barely showed any emotion on the outside, but take a closer look, you could see her eyes flashing with righteous indignation. Those who know her know she's a moral force, and a natural leader. She had the entire community unified behind her. Her arguments were damning: fair housing violations, environmental fraud, procedural corruption in the zoning process. For Olympus' infinite legal budget, we were in real trouble.

Nicole and I had a few informal, off-the-record chats. Lawyers are like this. They fight in court, they let their clients sort out the consequences, but then they go to the bar or play golf together when the day's over. She approached me once.

"Sen., you're too good for this." she started. "Ever considered stopping selling your soul to corporations and fight for the good guys?"

She said it half-jokingly. But the question felt like a punch. "Too good for this"? I tried to give her a simple answer. "I could use the money and connections, Nicole. I won't work for them forever. I want to work in criminal law."

"Criminal law? You want to fight for justice?" Nicole continued, now seeming intrigued. "Then you have nothing to do here. You shouldn't fight for a corrupt company like Olympus."

Inside, I was burning with rage. Listen to that patronizing tone. Who are you, to pass down judgment? I tried to stay calm, but I could feel the heat rise in my face. And she must've seen it, because she instantly apologized. "Sorry, I didn't mean it. I'm sure you have your reasons." She said in her usual, matter-of-fact tone.

Alright, she wants to know my reasons? I'd show her what her righteous cause is built on.

"Why don't I show you something, Nicole?" I asked. "Do you have the subcontractors ledger?"

During discovery, Olympus turned over truckloads of documents, hidden in there was a ledger with over 1,000 subcontractors. Most were shell companies, but there was a single name I had in mind, Evelyn C. I looked up the address, and drove Nicole there.

It's a tiny, struggling depot in Riverside. We didn't go in, but from afar, we watched Evelyn working inside, her three young boys playing in the lot next to a yellow excavator.

"This is Evie, 43, a single mother of three..." I explained to her. "She runs a small demolition company... that she inherited from her dead husband."

Nicole blinked at me. I found the news article on my phone and passed it to her. "Her husband died two years ago, in a construction accident unrelated to Olympus. Now, all she has is a mountain of debt and this scrap of a business."

I brought up some chat logs and showed it to her as well, letting everything sink in. "She's been calling our office non-stop, messaging me every day. She kept asking me when the construction's going to start, and how the lawsuit is going. Do you know why?

"Evie risked everything to secure a $4 million contract for the Olympus Towers. As I understand it's a desperate bid. She mortgaged the few assets she had. The contract would be 95% of her projected revenue for the next 5 years. But she won't get paid until construction starts."

I watched Nicole closely, how the self-righteousness was draining out of her face. "Nicole, you think you're on the side of justice? But if you win this class-action, Evie loses the contract. She defaults on her loan. She loses her business. She loses her home and her ability to feed the kids."

I leaned closer. "Evie has a documented history of depression and self-harm attempts after her husband passed. Do you think she'd survive losing everything this time? You're willing to push her over the edge? You save a building, but you'll put her children through a pain you can't even imagine."

"But the community center…" began Nicole. "The community also needs the clinic and—"

"Get off your high horse. You don't want to help the community. You just want to hurt Olympus." I could taste the venom in my voice. "I know your mentor. He doesn't care about an injunction. He's trying to get a massive settlement so he can become the local hero. You know that to be true." She held my eyes, but remained silent. "But if something happens to this woman, who would take responsibility? Will you?

"So no, Nicole," I straightened up. "I don't sympathize with your cause. You think I'm a corporate puppet? That's your shallow judgment. I couldn't care less about Olympus' quarterly report. I thought this through deeply, and I've made my decision. Between the community center and Evie, I'm choosing her. I'm doing this for her family."

I know I hit her hard that day, she was absolutely stunned. She said nothing on the return trip.

We spoke a few more times after that. She was troubled. But she was also less judgmental, and more searching. She was softer, trying to find a middle ground, maybe a redesign, something that doesn't involve a permanent injunction. She could not abandon her job, but her conviction was fractured. She made some procedural errors—I'm not sure if they're intentional or not—that proved fatal. In the end, we won the appeal.

Anyway, I hope you learned a lesson, dear Reader, like Nicole did. Am I a dirty corporate lawyer? A lot of people might think so. But sometimes the most ethical choice is the one that looks the worst on paper.

* * *

The story could've stopped there. But as it turned out, Nicole still didn't learn her lesson. A month later, I was leaving the headquarters when I ran into her again. She was waiting for me, and this time, she was furious. Her whole body shaking.

"You... you lying piece of shit." She hissed. "You lied to me, you little prick? I just visited Evie. Her husband isn't even dead!? He's perfectly alive and well! You made it all up? The tragedy? The suicide risk?"

"Her husband is alive, yes." I replied. "I don't know about her suicide risks, though. I never actually spoke to that woman."

"What... what about the chat logs? And the news article?"

"What news article?" I smiled. "Chat logs? I don't remember it."

She stared at me with disbelief. "You... you lying scumbag! That was professional misconduct and you're going to pay for this!"

"Nicole, why does it matter? You couldn't have won either way."

"No, we could've won! You think we couldn't? I could've objected to a number of evidence. We had a solid case! We had a good cause... we could've gotten a bigger settlement if not for you. We lost because of your dirty tricks!"

"I know. Brilliant, right?" I smiled wider. "Not many lawyers could've pulled that off."

She stared at me, for the first time I knew her she was at a loss for words. "I thought you were a good lawyer, but you sold your soul to them already? And look at you, look at how smug you are. Did they at least pay you well? Are you happy with yourself?"

"They paid me very well, and I'm very happy about it. But more than that, I'm happy because of you."

"Why? You're saying you enjoyed manipulating me?! You enjoyed taking advantage of my sympathy?"

"You're getting all the wrong ideas. Very well. You want to know why, is that it? You want to know why I'm really doing this? You needed only to ask. Allow me to tell you why, then. You deserve to hear it."

I walked a few steps to the side, looking off at the horizon. "I couldn't care less about Olympus or the money. Why am

I so happy right now? Ah, it's because… you see, 'I have a dream'!"

"You have a what?"

The Senator has a dream

I have a dream. That one day, people will no longer be judged by the color of their skin, nor by their character or actions, nor by their backgrounds, their beliefs, their opinions, or "which side they're on."

Nor will they be judged by social media. Nor will they be judged by journalists. Nor will they be judged by news media.

No, no, no. I have a dream, that one day, everyone will only be judged by three things: **evidence, proof, and the law!**

It's as it should be! A world that doesn't run on feelings, but on principles. A world based not on personal bias, but on facts. A world that is finally 100% fair. A world that will know true justice! Finally, there will be no more discrimination. No more cancel culture. No more mob rules!

It'd be the perfect world! And you know the worst people standing in my way? Not Olympus. Not even the criminals. It's people like you, Nicole, who are corrupting the legal system from the inside out! With your self-righteousness, your feelings, and your empathy! What is the purpose of the legal system? It's to remove human bias and personal feelings. It's to defend civilization from self-appointed moralists like you!

Yet you think you can bypass the whole legal process just based on your intuition? You imagine you are God, capable of judging which innocent person deserves to be saved? That you're capable of weighing the life of "Evie" against the interests of thousands of people in the community? Unscrupulous lawyers like you are the reason the world is going to shit, and I'm doing God's work by striking you down!

You think you know **the truth** about Evie? You know nothing! Yes, I fabricated her story. **But it could've been true.** In that list of 1,000 contractors, how do you know there weren't 10, 20, even 30 "Evies"? Contractors whose livelihoods hang by a thread? What then, Nicole? Are you going to switch sides again? You'll never know the full picture. **That's why truth is unknowable, and it's irrelevant.** That's why the justice system isn't about truth. It's about **fairness**. Because the least we can have is a **fair fight**! Where both sides present their strongest possible cases. That's why a lawyer's job is to do whatever possible to win for their client!

I represented my client to the absolute best of my ability. But you? You failed. You could've won easily, but you lost, because of your "empathy"? Do you know what that means? **What you call "empathy" is nothing more than a condescending form of pity.** It's a narcissistic, self-congratulatory emotion that changes depending on which sad soul is right in front of you. It means you lack principle and you cannot be trusted with making decisions. It's proof enough you didn't care about justice. You just enjoyed the feeling of being the one who swoops in to "save" them, whoever it is.

A normal person with empathy is pitiful, it means they're prone to manipulation. A lawyer with empathy is no lawyer at all. When you choose your "feelings" over your duty, you fundamentally failed as a law professional.

The law is sacred! **The law is inherited wisdom built on generations of suffering, revisions, and repairs. It's the culmination of millennia of human struggle.** It is a gift. Every single article and amendment was a response to some past human failing, so we don't endlessly repeat our mistakes. It's the only thing worthy of protection and respect. And you want to throw it all out and replace it with your flawed judgment? Over my dead body!

And how do I feel? Oh, I feel great, that I finally wiped that disgusting self-satisfied expression off your face. Lawyers like you make me want to puke. And you're just the beginning. I'm going to take great pleasure in defeating, humiliating, eradicating all of you! You're a disgrace! Now get out of my sight and don't let me see you again!

* * *

With that, I finished my speech. Nicole—she didn't move. She just stared, her face a mask of shock and dawning horror. It took her a full minute before she slowly turned and walked away without a word. Her steps not exactly steady.

A small legal victory? But I consider it a major step for humanity. We're now one step closer to true fairness and true justice!

The law isn't about justice

I have a dream to eliminate injustice from the world, but perhaps I could use your help. You want to do good in this world, but now you're wondering what "good" even means, and what we can believe in? The answer is obvious, isn't it? The answer is **you can believe in the collective wisdom that is the law.**

Professor Marylowe thinks the majority are passive, harmless idiots. But he's wrong. The majority is dangerous, because idiots are dangerous. That's why you wear seatbelts. Because deep down, you know other people are not to be trusted. You know the world is full of drunk and blind morons. Do you disagree? Do you claim to believe in the goodness of humanity? Then stop wearing seatbelts and I'll see how long you'd last.

The law provides the only sanctuary from the tyranny of the mob. That's why we don't live in a democracy. We live in a democratic republic. We have the Constitution, the Bill of Rights, the Electoral College... precisely to stop majority rule.

Some people say, "Yes, the law is not perfect. But it's the best we have." That is nonsense. The law is perfect. The problem is most people fundamentally misunderstand the purpose of the law.

I had this conversation with Marylowe's postdoc, Alison, once. As a physicist, she is quite intelligent, but with misplaced ideals. We were talking about a murder case in the lodge we were staying at. I was representing the suspect. She was apparently feeling lost, and she asked me:

"What if [the suspect] actually murdered someone, would you still defend him?"

"Of course I would," I replied. "So what, murderers don't deserve to be defended?"

"That's not what I meant... What I meant was... Would you still use your legal loopholes and everything to try to get him a lighter sentence? Or even get him to go free? I mean, maybe you've already done it last time when you helped two suspects go free. How would you feel if one of them is actually a murderer?"

I paused for a second. "It doesn't matter," I said. "What really matters is whether the prosecutors had enough evidence to prove they committed murder. And they couldn't. There wasn't enough proof to convict them, so they need to go free. It's as simple as that."

"And it doesn't bother you that your whole job is based on a flawed system?"

"Flawed?" I remembered smiling. "How so? It's the perfect system."

"But you literally just proved justice is not law. That within your system, criminals could go free. If they did a good job covering their tracks."

She's quite sharp, isn't she? But do you see the flaw in her reasoning?

It's that she, like many others, thinks the law is about enforcing justice, or about discovering truth. This is completely wrong. **The law has nothing to do with justice or truth, and it shouldn't be.**

If justice is what you want, you don't need law. You just need an angry mob. Give them each a pitchfork. The ensuing justice is much more swift and satisfying.

There was an imperial Chinese scholar who witnessed the Nuremberg Trials. He went back home, told everyone about it, and nobody believed him. They asked, "Why were war criminals given a trial at all?" Imagine if it were Imperial China. What would happen to these criminals? They'd be instantly whipped and branded. Their tongues cut off. Slow-sliced to pieces. Quartered. Boiled to death in hot tar. Stoned to death by the mob. Their whole families buried alive.

And none of it came with a fair trial. They're criminals anyway. Everyone knows they're criminals. They deserve whatever's coming to them. Kill them, cut them to pieces, torture them. Nobody would object. Everyone would only celebrate it. You're doing the world a favor.

But is this a world you want to live in? Imperial China?

No. The law is not here to enforce justice. The law is here to do the exact opposite. The law is put in place to stop the chaos that is the mob. It's to stop charismatic anarchists like Raymond Marylowe.

That's why I defend criminals. It's because the system itself needs to be held accountable. Because that's the only thing that separates us from Imperial China.

7

Justice Is Winning (According To The Criminal Defense Lawyer)

What the law? The law is the meaning of life. It's an ancestral gift. It's the only thing worthy of respect and protection.

Some law might rub you the wrong way. They might not make logical sense. But the Life of the Law has never been logic or idealism. The law is inherited wisdom based on experience. I repeat: **experience**. The law is a treasure trove of collective wisdom of all human history. Every piece of wisdom was created as a reactive measure for some tragedy or crime that happened in the past. And laws were put in place to prevent such tragedies from happening again. To forget the law is to forget their suffering. It's to say the victims' sacrifices were in vain, it's to say their lives, their existence, were meaningless. It is anti-human.

If you don't respect the law, what do you believe in instead?

Logical reasoning? Numbers and statistics? No. Not when there are people like Marylowe around, who can twist logic any way he wants. He's a scientist who doesn't even believe in truth? Maybe even he has given up trying to find the truth? What then? Narcissistic empathy and fleeting emotions? No, of course not. Humanity would sooner go extinct. People with "empathy" or "sense of justice" are the easiest to manipulate. They're the source of all mob rule.

Other than the law, there is nothing else. There is no alternative. So now you know what "truth" is: **truth is what's determined in court**. And now you know what "justice" is: **justice is winning**.

Master the system

It's a shame very few people understand this principle, even lawyers. I remember briefly considered applying for a certain elite law school. Two years before the application deadline, I decided to interview the application officer to understand the process. About an hour later, I was just drilling him about their marking criteria for the personal essay, when he sighed and cut me off.

"Sen.," said the admission officer, Mr. Thompson, trying for a paternal tone. "I can tell you're trying to **game the system.** Honestly? Don't. Just be honest, be yourself. Especially during the interview and with your personal statement, we want to see you as a person, not a set of perfectly optimized metrics."

I felt my blood run cold. I should've left right there, but I was young and hot-headed. So I went ahead. "Gaming the system?" I asked. "Mr. Thompson, I gave you an hour of my time to test the integrity of your admission process, but it seems to me you have no respect for your own rules. What you said was philosophically obscene."

"I... I'm not sure I follow."

"The appeal to an unwritten, emotional standard beyond established rules is the single most dangerous idea in human history. I want you to answer carefully: by using that phrase, 'gaming the system', you're implying there's something other than the system. If so, what is it?

"Because the system is in place to eliminate prejudice and discrimination. Is that not right? So I wanted to respect it as much as possible. But you're telling me to not do it? Are you admitting your system is not adequate to prevent discrimination? That there is discrimination in your selection process?

"'Be honest?' But who decides who's honest? Are you a lie detector? If so, why don't you patent yourself and make trillions of dollars? 'Interview?' Is that the less defined process where you allow for prejudice and discrimination to enter?

"No? But if the system is adequate, the personal element is redundant. If the system is inadequate, you must be introducing bias to compensate. Which is it?"

He stared at me as he searched for his words, as he realized there was no good answer. Obviously there wasn't. He was about to open his mouth again when I decided I had enough. I told him to keep his mouth shut before incriminating his institution any further, and I stood up and left. I decided it's not the right college for me.

The bottom line is this: there is no such thing as "gaming the system," because it implies there is something other than the system. The reality is, there is nothing other than the system. **There is only the system.** To think otherwise is disrespecting the system.

Morality is a disease

Morality is the worst thing you could've had. Let's illustrate this with the example of a fictional trial. Let's say it's early 1900s in small town Alabama. Let's say a black man—call him Tom Robinson—is accused of raping a white woman—call her Mayella Ewell. And the accuser was her father, Bob Ewell.

Tom claimed he was caught in the wrong place at the wrong time. But his real misfortune is that he got the worst criminal defense lawyer in history, a certain Atticus Finch.

The crimes of Atticus Finch are many. He decided to defend Tom Robinson not because it's his job as a lawyer, but because he believed in Tom Robinson's innocence. He claimed to know the truth. He thought he was the all-knowing God.

I hope you're not as conceited as him. Asking "did the defendant actually commit the crime?" is the single most useless, time-wasting activity you could've done. It's the same category as asking "Does God exist?"

Evidence may be fabricated or planted by the prosecutors. Witnesses lie. Lawyers are not God. We cannot travel to the past to find the real truth. In this case, only two people might actually know the "truth," and that's Tom and Mayella. But we cannot read their minds. So truth is unknowable. And because it's unknowable, it is irrelevant.

It's not even about presumption of innocence. It's that "truth" is fundamentally meaningless. A criminal is someone who is found guilty in court. That's all there is. When a lawyer thinks he has the "truth" and "justice" on his side, what does he do? He becomes complacent, like Finch did. Finch gave a grand speech and lectured the jurors on "doing the right thing". Excuse me? What does that have to do with the case!? He's so busy playing the hero that he abandoned his client. That's what happens when you prioritize being a "good person" over doing your job.

Worse, what if the lawyer thinks their client is guilty? Their "empathy" and "sense of justice" evaporate. That's when they offer a half-hearted, weak defense, convinced that they're serving a greater good by ensuring the "guilty" man is punished. They become the judge, the jury, and the executioner, all because they're deluded in thinking they could ever know the truth.

In a perfect world, such a lawyer would be disbarred immediately. Or they should stick to working in some backward Alabama swamp, like Finch. The real tragedy, however, is that this amateur somehow inspired a whole generation of other lawyers. Many of them see him as their "hero." And now these lawyers are corrupting the justice system from the inside out. If this trend continues, it'd be the end of the civilization as we know it.

That said, I'm almost pleased to hear many recent lawyers were inspired by Jimmy McGill, or Saul Goodman. This is someone who weaponizes the law for his own gain, which is all wrong. But his methods are sound, and he's infinitely better than Atticus Finch.

What the Senator would've done

"Alright, Senator. So Nicole is bad, that admission officer is bad, now Atticus Finch is also bad. Saul Goodman is not bad

*but also not good… Why don't you demonstrate what a good lawyer is supposed to be like? Let's just take Tom Robinson's case for example. What would **you** do in that situation?"*

Ah, what would I do? Let's entertain the scenario.

I'd immediately start a PR campaign exposing the Ewells of incest, bible-burning, being communist sympathizers and Union sympathizers. The name Ewell would be whispered in the whole Alabama with disgust and hatred. And that's only the start.

I'd then immediately have Tom Robinson go through a surgical castration. How could he have committed rape if he lacked his instrument? At least, the jury would no longer see him as a threat. Now, everyone sees him with pity and sympathy. The threat is neutralized, why not let him go?

And don't forget, it's a small town, I know the jury members. Does Mr. Tate's son have a gambling problem? I can help wipe that out. Or I can make sure they escalate the debt collection. Perhaps Mr. Cunningham's wife is having an affair with the postman? I'll help you destroy him with lawsuits, or I'll expose the affair to the whole town. Mr. Jones needs a loan to keep his farm afloat? I can either help you secure the loan, or I'll make sure they foreclose the farm and you can starve on the street. Make your choice wisely.

I'd hire at least three expert witnesses. One phrenologist to testify that Bob Ewell has the skull shape of a congenital liar. One psychoanalyst to diagnose Mayella with a textbook case of female hysteria. Finally, one fire-and-brimstone priest to declare he has seen into Tom Robinson's soul, and it's as pure as snow. And anyone who dares vote against an innocent man would guarantee eternal damnation in hell for themselves, their children, and their children's children.

Atticus Finch gives a grand speech about "Do the right thing" and "All men are created equal." He appeals to the goodness of humanity. It demonstrates a pitiful, pathetic understanding of human nature. Humans are not good. You don't influence people by appealing to their good conscience. You influence them by greed and by fear. You fight prejudice with bigger prejudices.

And of course Finch lost the case. What did he do afterwards? Nothing. He shrugged it off and blamed it on the "prejudice" of the townspeople. He convinced himself there's nothing to be done. He packed his briefcase and walked home to read the newspaper.

The newspaper! Your client was found guilty because of you! You think I'd waste my time reading the newspaper? No. I would've won that case. Tom Robinson would've walked free. Even if the odds were a million to one against me, I would burn that town to the ground before I admit defeat. I would salt the earth. When I'm done, Maycomb, Alabama would be nothing but a smoking crater on the map. That's the price of crossing me.

"But Senator... your plan is to blackmail the jurors? Bribe the witnesses? Mutilate the defendant? How is that not breaking the laws?! You're committing crimes!"

Nonsense. I would never break the law. You really think I'd leave evidence around? You really think you can catch me? That you can prove beyond a reasonable doubt that I'm guilty?

And if you can't prove it in court, then it's not breaking the law, is it?

8

WHAT CAN YOU BELIEVE IN, REALLY?

Professor Raymond Marylowe: Jeez, what a lunatic! I almost forgot that about him. Alright, let's move on.

Whether it's God, whether it's a lawyer like the Senator, whether it's the philosophers of the old, whether it's a theoretical physicist like me, what everyone can agree on is this one thing:

Truth is unknowable. And since it's unknowable, as the Senator said, **truth is also irrelevant.**

This is the fundamental axiom from which the whole world can be derived. If you had one take-away message from this book, **this is the one.** Because this is the single most important lesson you must take to heart. I know I said this about something else, but that wasn't it. This is it. This is the real message, that **there is no such thing as objective truth.** 99.99% of the people in the world do not understand this. That's why they're all trapped. But as you truly let go of the idea of truth, you will be free.

But you have to believe in something, right? So the obvious question is, **in such a world, what can you believe in?**

There are really only three sensible answers to this.

- **The first answer is religion.**

- **The second answer is the law.**

Both can give you true coherence. Any other answers are hypocritical and self-contradictory. But both are crutches. You free yourself of doubt and insecurities, but you lose freedom.

Do you know the third answer, smart reader? Obviously, that is my answer! Allow me, Professor Raymond Marylowe, to answer that question for you through a real-life story!

I wish I could show you the video, because it's one of the most important videos in the entire world, and just watching it once can change your life, so it may as well be my sacred scripture. But let me recount to you what happened. A number of years ago. I was giving lectures at the ICTP Summer School, and I wandered off into town for a while, and I saw a sanitation worker working on the street. But then I saw this:

A dog is latched onto a garbage collector's leg, growling and barking. The man walks on, dragging the dog with him, but the dog holds on. The man shouts and shakes his leg, but the dog holds on and continues to try to bite through the man's pants. The man kicks the dog with his other leg—the dog holds on. The man takes out a can of pepper spray and sprays at the dog—the dog still holds on. The man swings his dog-attached leg into a tree trunk, but the dog still won't let go. The man finally tries to pry the claws off, but the dog bites down on his hand. Eventually, the dog wins, overwhelming the man, pinning him to the ground, mauling and biting him all over.

Later I learned it's a dog with rabies. But at that time, I didn't know that. I just thought, look over there, that's the dog version of Raymond Marylowe. I never thought I needed to be understood. But at that moment, I did feel... something. Like a kinship.

And now, I hope that becomes the dog version of you too, dear Reader. Someone honest, authentic, and free. Listen, it doesn't matter what you believe in, **as long as you believe in yourself and no one else.**

Of course, a lot of other people have said, "Believe in yourself." But they never taught you how. But now you know how. If you choose to believe in yourself, then go all the way. Truly believe in yourself. Identify a goal—whatever it is, it doesn't matter—and then you just **bite**. Don't ask questions, don't ask for permission, don't wait for a good time to start. Instead, commit to it fully. Be like the dog. That's how I was able to defeat the Senator in court! Hahaha, you really think anyone other than me could've done it?

Live your own truth

When I say "greatest investor in the world," who do you think of immediately? Warren Buffett, isn't it? But his return isn't even that good. So how did he get that title? There's no higher authority granting titles like that. Of course—he anointed and appointed himself! Who else was going to do it for him? The former greatest investor in the world? His mother?

No, there is no one else. You know Warren Buffett as the greatest investor in the world, because Warren Buffett made a point of telling everybody that Warren Buffett is the greatest investor in the world.

He created a truth out of thin air, and he imposed it onto the world until it becomes a reality.

But that's exactly what you should do. If you wait around for someone to discover your amazing ability, for the people around you to lift you up, you're going to wait a very long time! You might think you **are** amazing, and you **deserve** to be recognized as such. But objective truth is unknowable, and it is irrelevant. If you wait for people to arrive at the "correct" conclusion, they will never do. You need to impose your reality onto others. So what if they push back? What exactly makes their truth more valid than your truth? Nothing!

And you need to **tell, not show.** If Warren Buffett just showed people his amazing investment portfolio, and let people reach their own conclusion, what would people do? Well, 90% won't reach any conclusions, because they probably can't even read numbers! And the 10% will probably arrive at the wrong conclusions. "Wow, Warren Buffett is truly the **luckiest** investor in the world!" or "Warren Buffett is truly the **smartest** investor in the world!" Listen, if you sit around waiting for things to happen—either nothing will happen at all, or something will happen but they won't go your way. You need to be pro-active!

You must take full responsibility of your life

People talk about this like it's some profound duty. It's not.

You need to take full responsibility of your life. Why? Because the majority of the people are idiots! If you don't take care of yourself, who will? Are you going to trust these idiots to do it? Who can you trust? Nobody!

You must become self-reliant

A lot of young people at university want socialism, but not the "state ownership of productions" type of socialism. What they really want comes down to one thing: **welfare!** Things like affordable healthcare, investments in housing, more government protections and unions, Universal Basic Income when AI inevitably replaces humans.

Listen, I'm telling you this because I care about you and I love you. You must absolutely reject welfare and UBI. You don't even need to be a savant in geopolitics. It's based on a very simple, brain-dead proof. In order for me to believe in welfare, I must believe:

- Politicians and corporations care about me.

- Politicians have to give me money (after all, they need me and my votes, right?)

- Politicians are kind and empathetic people, they will make sure I don't starve because it's the right thing to do. They have my best interests in mind.

- Politicians are competent with money—they're good with collecting, managing, and distributing it.

- Politicians are competent with implementing massive social programs, they'll make sure I always get my due on time.

I'm sorry, but **are you stupid?!** If you believe in any single one of them, then you deserve to starve to death when they inevitably forget a monthly payment. Because politicians are all stupid! And they don't even see you as humans, just Homer Simpsons. Listen, work at McDonald's if you have to, work as a plumber, it doesn't matter. But never fall into the trap of getting welfare, it's a death sentence!

How to respect other people's autonomy

A reader who's a salesperson wrote to me. *"Professor, I'm working on a franchise that focuses on building Generational Leverage and residual income. Both me and my distributors have the same problem: we have trouble making cold calls. We feel bad disturbing people when they're going about their days. What do we do?"*

First of all, you're playing God thinking you are disturbing people. Secondly, it's not up to you to reinforce people's boundaries! They made the decision to post their personal information to a public database, they made the decision to use a smartphone and plug into the "system." They have nothing to complain about!

Nobody can cold call me even if they try to, you know why? Because I use a flip phone, which I wrap in aluminum foil so no one can reach me! Getting "unsolicited" calls is a choice they made. They could opt out any time they want to.

"Should I treat others like I want to be treated?" Why should you? Remember the lesson about personal responsibility? When you step over the line and attempt to "fix" their lives, it's worse than being disrespectful. You're erasing their personal identity and denying their autonomy! God has given them free will to make decisions, and you're robbing them of that opportunity? For what? Just so you don't feel uncomfortable?

Yes, I can tell. You don't want to make cold calls not because you're considerate. But because rejections make you confront your own inadequacy. You're still letting others judge you, as such you're still viewing others as your God. You need to find your own God, like the dog. Does the dog care about rejection, embarrassment, pain, or humiliation? Exactly!

Finally, Embrace Ugliness

This is undoubtedly the single most important lesson in the whole book. Because it really isn't a new lesson. This is the whole book and the whole world.

- The world is an ugly place? Of course it is.

- Look at the average person who is lazy, gullible, and petty, is it not an ugly sight? Of course it is.

- Governments commit atrocities, and people are complacent. Is it not ugly? It's very ugly.

- Rule-breakers breaking ethical and moral boundaries without consequences. Is it not a display of ugliness? It's very ugly.

- Corporations destroying local community centers purely to satisfy their greed. Is that not ugly? It's ugly.

- Scientists twist virtues into pathologies and elevate pathologies to virtues by clever rhetoric and cherry-picking evidence. Is it not ugly? Yes, it is.

- Lawyers twisting the law to justify their own ideal, while justice is corrupted beyond recognition. Is that not ugly? Yes, it is.

It's all very ugly. But what can we do about it? Shall we try to change people? Shall we lead them to a better life? Should we work together to make the world a more beautiful place?

Don't delude yourself. Are you not one of such ugly creatures yourself? You, me, everyone else. Are we not all driven by greed, fear, and self-interests? Can selfish, narcissistic, biased, short-sighted creatures like us really judge good from bad? No, we cannot.

In fact, how do you know being ugly isn't a good thing? Because it is.

You need to realize one thing about the world. The world is never built on goodness, or compassion, or altruism.

No. What really makes the world go around is greed, jealousy, lust, and competition. These are simply much more powerful motivators than any virtues.

Companies aren't producing life-saving drugs out of the goodness of their heart. Doctors aren't treating you because they're compassionate. Technological advancements did not happen because the tech CEOs want to make the world a better place. All these happened because of people's greed. The Space Race was fueled by jealousy. The French Revolution was a reign of fear. Laws were created only following some past tragedy and atrocity.

Everything you find "good" today comes from a place of ugly. The ugly side of humans is the true driving force behind all societal and technological advancement. So this is the one thing you need—**Embrace ugliness.** This is it.

Love the ugly side of human nature. See the beauty in it. Accept it. Live it. Embrace it.

- Embrace your selfishness.

- Embrace your ambition.

- Embrace your desire.

- Embrace your lust.

- Embrace your jealousy.

Only then will you be honest with yourself. Only then will you rid yourself of the hypocrisy and self-doubt that's trapped you all your life. Only then will you finally be free and finally be happy. Because how can you be happy if you hate 100% of the population? You can't.

You'll be successful too, because finally, nothing will hold you back. And who knows? You might even add some value to the world. And make your own life and the lives of your loved ones better.

9

Professor's Practical Q&A Session

Here are some practical lessons for you to help you truly internalize the BBB philosophy.

"Professor, how do I develop social skills?"

Only stupid people need social skills. How does one develop social skills, really? At the very core, social skill is developed through one thing: **compromise**. It's like in physics, when two bodies collide, they must negotiate on a new path. If you're smart enough, then you never have to compromise, and you won't have to develop social skills!

"Professor, how do I get people to respect me?"

Ugh, wrong question. Why didn't you ask "How to get obedience"? And if people don't respect you, so what? What can they do? Is it illegal? Can they throw you in jail? There is nothing they can do!

Hopefully, you no longer crave the respect of the "masses," but maybe you still want respect from your friends? In that case, know that respect comes from winning. But what's the first necessary component of winning? You need enemies! If you don't have enemies, how are you going to "win"? So the first step is that you need to stop seeing people as friends. Start seeing them as enemies. Then you don't care about their respect. If anything, you want them to under-estimate you!

"Professor, how do I deal with hate?"

Don't worry about hate and don't hate others. What is hate really? Short of the desire to take revenge, the number one source of hatred in the world is **jealousy**.

Back when they tried to destroy Assange's reputation, they immediately accused him of sexual assault. But why sexual assault of all things? It makes sense that it'd make women hate him. But why does it work so well on men as well? The reason, of course, is that it makes men jealous. That's right—**jealousy** is the number one reason behind all the hate in the world. It's the single most Ugly Emotion in the World.

By the way, the Jealousy Card is actually the one thing that works even better on women than on men. Because it's mostly men who are jealous of other men. But for women? Both men and women are jealous of them. The one thing that makes people most jealous? Effortless success from privilege. Now that you know how jealousy works, go use this card to destroy other people, but don't let it get to you!

"Professor, what if I'm feeling lost in life?"

Find one thing and get very good at it. It doesn't matter what it is, but make sure you're the top of the top. Because then you get close to the truth, you see through people's lies and you can deduce why they're lying to you, and that tells you how the world really works. But to get there, you still need audacity.

I remember back in that career summit, I walked into a conversation of a student complaining.

"Everyone! I applied to 1,800 entry-level jobs with the help of AI last month, got two group interviews. One ended in disaster because I didn't have three years of experience. The other one agreed to hire me, except they wanted me to work 60 hours a week! I refused to work such exploitative hours, and now my parents are saying I'm the problem and I should just get any job so I can move out? Am I the problem, or is late-stage capitalism broken!?"

"Clearly you're the problem," I said as I sat down. "60 hours is nothing. I was about 20 when I was working 100 hours a week for months. I was living in the university library, lost consciousness a few times from lack of sleep, nearly died of heart failure a couple of times. My doctor told me if I didn't stop, I'd die for real. For once in my life, I thought about giving up. But then I thought to myself, 'Wait a minute, if I die from something so stupid, then I deserve to die!' And so I didn't quit and I pulled through. Eventually, I made it. And these days I don't work at all because I've got a permanent contract. Do you feel I'm privileged? But it's my karmic reward for risking my life!"

"That's so stupid!" a student replied. "Even if you did succeed, it has nothing to do with risking your life. Don't you understand diminishing returns? If you work more than 40 hours a week, your productivity drops! You could've had better results and work-life balance if you worked smarter!"

"Yeah? If you stop working, your productivity drops to 0! How is that smart? Let me tell you something: in reality, working smart is working dumb, and working dumb is working smart. A lot of people think the more you work, the more tired you get, but that's nonsense. In reality, the more you work, the more energized you get. It's called Newton's First Law—the law of momentum! And unlike dumb economic laws like 'diminishing returns,' this is a real, smart, physicist law.

"People like you get tired not because you work too much, but because you worry too much. Worrying about 'productivity,' 'work-life balance,' 'am I doing the smart thing?', 'am I being efficient?', 'am I being exploited?' Who cares? Only dumb people care. I never ask myself those questions, because I never doubt myself, because I'm too amazing. And guess what? They never exploit people like me. They only exploit people like you with low self-esteem. So yes, you deserve every problem you have. You brought them on yourself!"

"Professor, how to deal with trauma?"

You can't change the past, but you can prevent it from ever happening in the future by taking revenge. Senator said revenge is pointless and you gain nothing, but he's wrong. Revenge is boundaries. Like a while back, Matilda asked me, out of nowhere,

"Do you think I have the talent to become a good actor?"

I said, "What does talent have to do with it?"

"Well, do you think I'd become a great actor?"

"I hope not."

"How could you say that?! You mean you won't support me if I want to pursue a career in acting?!"

"What? Absolutely not! Why would I support something like that?!"

And she got quite mad! "Raymond! You're supposed to love me! You know, Katherine, our neighbor, her dream is to get into politics, but she had to stay at home all day to take care of her children, and she said it's her biggest regret. You wouldn't want me to live with regrets like this, would you?"

WHAT!? The bastard! As if Matilda didn't have enough crazy ideas already! Alright, eventually I averted the crisis, but it's out of the question to let such a behavior go unchecked, and I knew I needed to immediately take revenge on Katherine and her family. I went to have a chat with them, encouraged her to pursue her career in politics, and convinced her husband to support her. Mark my word, they're going to get a divorce before the year's out. And while they're busy, I'm going to convince their kids to go through gender-affirming treatments. That ought to teach that bastard a lesson on meddling with our affairs!

Anyway I asked Matilda to help me carry out the plan, but she said I was no fun, how it's always fighting people with me, and she wanted to do something nice instead. She doesn't understand it. Listen, you need to punish everyone who crosses you, take revenge no matter how minor the offense is!

"Professor, what if I'm addicted and distracted?"

You cannot be free if you have any addictions at all! So first of all, quit alcohol, drugs, and smoking. Then quit psychedelic drugs by firing your psychologist. Then quit digital addictions. Be like me and get a Nokia 2720 Flip phone. It has Google Maps and Gmail. What else do you need? Then you need to quit gambling, that includes trading stocks or bitcoins. It's what lazy people do when they sit around hoping good things happen to them, it's cowardice!

Then you should quit video games because it's a waste of time. A loser kid challenged me on this point once, "How is that wasting time? Everyone needs to relax! And why is watching movies so normalized, but there's so much stigma around video games? It's the same thing! And arguably it's even better than doomscrolling or partying! Video games are the 9th art! Have you seen the stories and the philosophy of these games?"

But he's right. It's no different from TV shows, or movies, or doomscrolling, or partying, or art, or philosophy. Because they're all stupid and wastes of time. But video games are the worst of them all, because they're also violent. And who told you you needed relaxing? Nobody needs relaxing, and you're not special. I can tell you're just being lazy!

Then you should quit pornography because it's the source of declining birth rates. People say it's because of economics and female education. But that's not true! In a world without porn, do you really think men would let poverty or feminism or the Me Too movement stop them from chasing women? No, they'd stop at nothing! The real culprit is pornography! So now birth rate plummeted, so countries import immigrants, which cause more political polarization, which will lead to the inevitable American civil war, and while their military is busy, everyone is going to invade everyone, which causes nuclear winter. The world is going to be destroyed, and whose fault is it? It's all pornography's fault!

"Professor, can you teach me a good pick-up line?"

Andrew asked me the same thing, let me paste my seduction lesson with him here.

* * *

"Fine... Let me now teach you the single best pickup line ever invented. Of course, it's created by none other than myself, and in all my years of using it, it has not failed me once. That's how scary and powerful it is. It works everywhere and anytime—daytime, nighttime, in a bar, on the street, whether she's standing, sitting, walking... It's objectively the best pickup line in the world, and possibly my best invention."

"It's so amazing? Can you... can you teach me?" asked Andrew.

"Alright, listen carefully... It goes like this. You ask her, 'Excuse me, can we swap shoes?'"

"'Can we swap shoes!?' What kind of line is that!? And... this is the best pickup line in the world?!"

"That's right. In the church business, a good pastor doesn't try to 'convert' people to his church. Instead, he looks up records of abuse and finds people at their most vulnerable stages. Similarly, you don't seduce women, you catch the vulnerable ones. Imagine a woman actually stops and reacts positively to a line like that? That's how you know she's susceptible."

"So it doesn't actually make them like you more?"

"Why do you want them to like you more?"

"But I just thought… seduction's more than that. This just sounds like gambling!"

"Exactly! The gambling aspect is what makes relationships so addicting and dopamine-inducing! That's why this line is so good. It maximizes efficiency, and you'll never go on a date with a time-waster again. So go."

"But wait, I'm not ready yet! What about after the pickup line? What do I even talk to women about? You know, I have no common language with them. All they do is gossip! There's even this lady called Bechdel who did a test about it, and she found two women literally can't have a single conversation without talking about another guy!"

"That's not true. They also talk about shoes and lipsticks and such. Now go."

"Wait, wait—one last question. What if I'm chatting with a woman and her boyfriend shows up? How do I deal with that?"

"You try to make him jealous. Because that makes him look bad and makes you look good."

"But what if he punches me?!"

"Punches you? Are you afraid of getting punched? Remember the Dog, Andrew. Go!"

"Wait. Let me see the dog video again…… Oh wow. I see now. This is so inspiring, Professor! I feel so inspired! I feel like I can take on the world!"

***

And then he went and had a ton of amazing successes all night! Anyway, read my book to find my full seduction lesson. For your own sake, though, I suggest you skip Matilda's seduction lesson. It's useless.

"Professor, I found a girlfriend, now what?"

After you find a partner, the #1 thing you need to focus on is to not get domesticated. Why is it that most relationships start with men in charge, but after 2-3 years of marriage, it always ends up with the women in charge?

Let me break it down for you. It's because women have three weapons. Their first weapon is food, because men rely on women for food, and because women can slow-poison the food. By the way, that's why I'm the one cooking for Matilda. Andrew thought I'm cooking because I got domesticated?! What an idiot! But look what happens when I cook. One of Matilda's greatest weapons—poof! Gone! Neutralized!

Their second weapon is sex, because men rely on women for sex. But not my relationship. Not that our private life is any of your business, but let's just say Matilda actually relies on me for sex!

Third is babies, because women can claim to speak for the babies, things like "You can't go out... your child needs you home!" Or "You can't stay at home... your child wants you gone!" That's why many smart men begin to take care of the babies and let their wives go out and work, so they seize control instead.

"Professor, what 'mindset' should I have?"

"If I'm afraid of failure, should I reframe failure? Should I tell myself 'I didn't fail. I just found one more thing that doesn't work'? 'It's not a failure if I learned something'? Should I stop asking myself, 'what if I fail,' and instead think 'what if I succeed?' Should I 'doubt my self-doubt?' 'What if my self-doubt is wrong?' Would 'abundance mindset' solve all my problems? But how do I develop it......"

Listen... The #1 problem of society today is we place too much importance on what's in our mind. Manifestation, motivations, visualization, therapy, psychology—it's all about minds, thoughts, feelings... but none of them matters!

1. Nobody knows your feelings, so they're not important to anyone else.

2. Your feelings are only important to you if you give them importance. They're no longer important if you ignore them.

Why do we care about our thoughts and feelings so much? It's because in the 1800s they invented the idea of "self-help" and "mindset," that you just need to sit under a tree, arrange your thoughts somehow, and this would somehow create some tangible shifts in the world and in your life. You can "Think and Grow Rich," and there is "Power in Positive Thinking."

Wouldn't that be great? No work required, but massive reward! Obviously lazy and cowardly people are going to love this idea! But reality is, the world doesn't operate on thoughts and feelings. The world operates on actions and initiative. The only thing that matters is your **behavior**.

For people who think "the mind is important because my feelings are real, my mental illnesses are real because they **feel** real." I made a flowchart for you:

Is there power in thoughts & feelings?

- YES → You manifested your mental illnesses and anxieties → Believe they don't exist to de-manifest them → Great, they're not important!

- NO → Great, they're not important!

People say *"Mindset is the operation system. How you think dictates how you act. Even what you're saying now about mindset not being important—isn't it a 'mindset' in itself?"*

Sure. In that case, the best mindset to have is to not have a mindset at all. But really, mindset is not an operation system. It's the contrary. **How you act dictates how you think.**

The dog doesn't read books about biting. The dog doesn't visualize it. The dog doesn't tell himself affirmations about attacking. The dog doesn't wonder "What if I fail?" or "What if I succeed?" The dog doesn't worry if he's as strong as the garbage man. The dog doesn't compare himself with other dogs. The dog just bites!

And once you overwhelm the garbage man, now your whole "mindset" about yourself changes instantly. You now have direct evidence you're stronger than a human! Your thoughts and feelings are a consequence of your action, not pre-requisites of it.

"Alright, Professor. But the dog is also of a different species, and it doesn't think at all! Are you saying we should stop thinking altogether? But I'm proud of my intellect and my rationality!"

Listen, thinking is not a sign of intellect. It's a sign you're not there yet. I never think, because—what do I need to think about? I already figured everything out. The reality is society has the completely backward idea of intellect. If you're the type who still thinks, read the next chapter.

10

How To Fix "Paralysis By Analysis" (a.k.a. Stupidity)

When I said "all labels are traps" I wasn't joking. Even words like "smart" are traps. Because everything everyone told you about being smart is wrong. I saw this idiotic quote once:

"Think of how stupid the average person is, and realize half of them are stupider than that."

But the quote is idiotic because they confused "average" with "middle." Probably because they are brainwashed by pseudo-science like psychology to think "IQ is a bell curve" (middle graph below).

But remember IQ is made up, intelligence doesn't have to be a bell curve. For example, psychologists could've made IQ tests easier. Then, most people would score high. Now we have a society where the majority of the people are smarter-than-average "geniuses" (left graph).

They could've made the test harder, so most people score low. In this society, the majority of the people are "stupid" (right graph).

Which is true? Who knows? You decide.

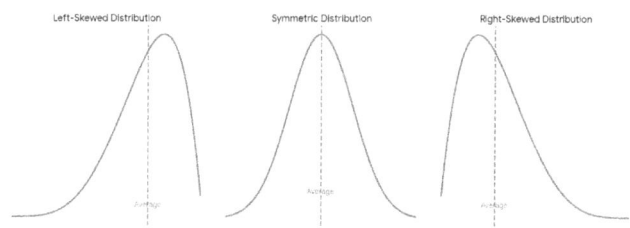

Other people compare IQs of sexes. "Men are better at certain tests, women at other tests. But on average, men and women have the same intelligence."

What a coincidence, right? What are the odds? But again, it's ridiculous. They **designed** the average IQ of both sexes to be the same. They can manipulate the outcome whichever way they want, by making certain tests harder/easier, and by scaling different tests differently.

So are men smarter than women, or are women smarter than men? I wouldn't be surprised either way. But really, we don't know! Nobody knows!

Some people have the idea, "I have a higher IQ, that means a better quality of life/more income/healthier life." Again it's wrong, statistics can't be applied to individuals.

IQ scale is also very misleading and manipulative. It makes people think intelligence varies by a lot. Your IQ might be 130, your friend might score 70. It looks like you're about twice as smart as your friend, because 130 is about twice of 70! Right?

How To Fix "Paralysis By Analysis"

But that's nonsense! Remember the scale is all made up! They defined the IQ cut-offs of most people to be between 70 and 130. But why 70 and 130? Why not 80 and 120? Why not 90 and 110? No reason. It's all made up.

They could've defined "stupid" to be 99, and "genius" to be 101. Now it doesn't look so different, does it? Now, it looks like you're only 2% smarter than your friend. In fact, you might even be dumber than your friend! It's very possible!

Listen, worrying about intelligence is stupid. I never care about people's intelligence, because I know none of them are smarter than me anyway. So what's the point of even thinking about it?

Another thing is most people got their idea of "smart" from media or books. But media are all stupid! For example, I've heard people say *Rick & Morty* is a very smart show, because Rick Sanchez is a theoretical physicist. I watched an episode—wait a minute, he's not even a theoretical physicist! He invented a portal gun—that's by definition an engineer! Are the screen writers stupid? They can't tell the difference between physicists and engineers? We theoretical physicists understand nature, we don't change it. Anyway, people see Rick being depressed and alcoholic and say, "See? Smart people are depressed. He's depressed because he's too smart." No... he's depressed because he's too stupid. If I was a dumb engineer pretending to be a physicist I'd be depressed too. And if he was smarter he'd have figured out how to be happy by now.

Anyway, that's what I'm talking about. All those writers in the entertainment industry have no real-life experience, so their creations are stupid. It's like how my postdoc Andrew likes American Psycho, apparently because he adores that sociopathic investment banker. But nothing about the banker seems like a real sociopath to me. It's clear to me the writer isn't a real sociopath, and doesn't even live or work in the sociopath circle, and really he's just writing things he knew nothing about. But that's the case with all these writers. They never even go outside, they know nothing of the world.

If you want to be smart, your first step is to stop watching stupid TV shows. For example, if you want smart TV shows, watch *The Big Bang Theory*. It features actual theoretical physicists, and it's very funny. And it's not sarcastic. By the way, here's how you instantly recognize stupid people: they are sarcastic. Sarcasm is the cheapest way to produce humor, because all you do is say the opposite of what you think, a monkey can do it. So it's for cowards who are too afraid of speaking their mind. That's why I'm never sarcastic. If you want to be smart and have Big Brass Balls you need to speak your mind too.

Anyway, sarcasm is another reason stupid people get depressed. Like the Gen-Z's, most of them can't handle how real and raw *The Big Bang Theory* is, and they watch that dumb show in the office where everyone's dysfunctional and hates each other. No wonder they're all depressed! If I watched dumb shows like that I'd be depressed too.

Some people say, *"Well, I'm smart and depressed. Because I see all the problems in the world that no one else sees! And it depresses me!"* Then why don't you go do something about it? *"Because I don't know how and people won't listen to me."* Ha, gotcha! You're not smart enough to figure it out!

Some say, "Smart people tend to overthink and over-analyze." No, only stupid people need to think about things. Truly smart people like me already know what to do, we can simply think after the fact. And the only thing I think about is how amazing I was just now.

Some people say, "Smart people see the meaningless of life." No, if you're smart, you see the meaning in everything. But for this one I blame the French. Listen, you need to get away from the French, they're all Negative Nancys. I know this because my college is right next to the French suburb. And I noticed this a long time ago, every single one of them loves to complain. They complain about everything. But mostly, they complain about other French people. And they also hate how French people are always unhappy and complaining so much, so they complain about the complaint culture in France. Anyway, how stupid is that? Whether you love the culture or hate it, you end up being sucked into it. You can't escape it, unless you literally, physically escape. You need to cut them all out.

The French once did the most good in the world, but are they proud? No. They're full of guilt, shame, and self-loathing. And they have no gratitude. They don't realize how fortunate they are. I went to Paris with Matilda and Andrew a while back, to do some luxury shopping. There's a bridge near the Eiffel Tower where a lot of guys are selling luxury brand products on their blankets. There were Hermès, Louis Vuitton, Prada, Gucci, Armani blazers and trousers, Chanel, Burberry, Rolex. If you go to elsewhere, they might cost thousands of euros or more. But over there, they're only €30–€300 each! Most were knockoffs. But some are genuine, you just have to know what to look for. For example, if you see glass shards inside the bags, or if you see price tags or protective tissue paper, they're all good signs. And Matilda is very good at spotting fakes. So we were having a lot of fun.

And then out of nowhere, someone screamed "Police! Police!" And so chaos erupted and everyone all started to run. Me and Matilda ran very fast and we got away. But Andrew was too slow because he's carrying all our stuff, and a thief on a motorcycle zoomed by and snatched two of the Dior bags he's carrying. Ugh. But still, at the end of the day, we got a bunch of luxury products for less than 1,000 euros, and we all found it quite thrilling and romantic. Where else could you have such a fun experience? But are the French happy with Paris or France? Not at all, all they do is to protest and complain. Every single French person is a pitiful existence except for the mathematicians. And that's a fact.

Even worse than the French are the Russians. If the French think criticizing things make them smart, Russians think being miserable somehow makes them deep. But in reality, these are all signs of stupidity. When smart Russian physicists write books, they're all extremely short and to the point. When Russian writers and philosophers write books they all write huge tomes. Do you see a pattern here? It's because the philosophers are stupid. If they're smarter they'd know how to express themselves more simply.

Some philosopher confronted me once, saying I committed "naturalistic fallacy." Basically, according to this philosopher, "What is natural isn't always good." Anyway I asked him, "What do you mean, 'naturalistic fallacy,' you mean there is more than one fallacy?"

And I looked it up... Oh my goodness, there are over 200 so-called logical fallacies! Most of these fallacies don't even have anything to do with logic, it's just linguistic! Listen, in reality there is only one logical fallacy, and that's called an incorrect argument, and if philosophers weren't complete idiots they'd be able to point out the incorrect argument, instead of having to invent 200 categories. They don't understand that real smart people—physicists, real scientists—always look for the **simplest** explanation, instead of the complex ones.

When someone complicates stuff, they're always hiding something. Most of the time they're hiding from the world that they're idiots. And what of these fallacies? "Whataboutism" is to hide from being a hypocrite. "Naturalistic fallacy" is to hide from being gay. "Ad hominem" is to hide from being unemployed.

When philosophers use big words, long sentences, and complex rhetorical devices, they think it makes them sound smart, but it only ends up trapping them. Their head becomes full of mental noises that they mistake with deep thinking. And these mental noises make them confused and paralyzed. And they couldn't do anything and end up becoming alcoholic. There's this Russian author whose books are all about "internal conflicts" that go nowhere. But internal conflicts are a sign of hypocrisy, so stop being a hypocrite. Anyway there's this clinical psychologist in the West who also loves to speak in confusing language, started talking about these books, got himself so confused that he developed a benzos addiction! It's just a further proof that stupidity gets you depressed.

"But isn't this book very philosophical?" But there are two types of philosophy:

1. **Existential**. Things like "what's the meaning of life" and interpretations of quantum mechanics. This is useless.

2. **Behavioral**. We figure out how people work and how systems work, and we deduce how we should behave. This is actually important.

I blame the limit of the English language for lumping together these two. In reality only idiots care about the first category of questions because nothing wastes your time more, and I suggest you spend 0 seconds of your life doing it.

In short, society doesn't know what intelligence is, so let me clarify. Being intelligent isn't about thinking deeply—a monkey can do that. It isn't about being confused and having internal conflicts—that's the opposite of intelligence. It's not about reading or "lifetime learning"—again, any idiot can do that and plenty of idiots do. All these aren't signs of intelligence. They are traps for the mediocre.

Being intelligent is about figuring things out. Once you figured things out, you wouldn't have to think anymore. You wouldn't have to discuss or debate anymore. And that's why I don't read books, they're all a waste of time, because I already figured out everything important. And if do want to read books, there are only three books you need: *Harry Potter*, *Don Quixote*, and my book, *The Physicist Detective vs. the Criminal Defense Lawyer*. 99.99% other books are useless and only make you overthink.

Listen, the world is very simple. Everything is simple cause and effect. And now that you read this book, you've figured it all out too, just like me! So for all intents and purposes you're now among the most intelligent people on the planet. You won't ever need to read another book again, so congratulations! Now go out there and do something, make me and the dog proud!

Afterword

I KNOW what you're thinking. You've seen the Senator in action, but what you really want is to see **me** in action! It's a great idea, so go read my memoir, *The Physicist Detective vs. the Criminal Defense Lawyer*. It's back when I was helping Scotland Yard solve impossible crimes all over the world with my physics knowledge. You also see how I masterfully won over Matilda from a phantom thief (ironic!), how I formed my Inner Circle, and how I fought all the legal battles with the Senator. And maybe, you'll see the growth journey of my two students, Andrew and Alison, and see yourself in them.

Ah, speaking of whom, here's Andrew. He's running towards me as we speak! Will you calm down? Why are you running?

"Professor... bad news! It's... it's about your book! *Big Brass Balls*? That you released a while back?"

Alright, Andrew, calm down and relax. Listen up, even if you go to an ER with your arm chopped off, they'll still have you wait 3–4 hours while they tend to people who are actually dying. So what are you concerned about? Wait, did Matilda read the book and discover how I want multiple wives? But it's impossible. She doesn't read books. She's sort of an idiot, which is why I like her.

"No, it's not Matilda... it's social media. They're calling your book toxic and offensive. Like when you call psychologists pseudo-scientists? And the people in the Mensa society 'mentally retarded'? They say it's inflammatory hate speech, and they're even calling for your book to be banned!"

Hahaha, of course they are. That just proves me right! You think I'd care if someone calls me a pseudo-scientist? Or call me mentally retarded? No, I wouldn't care, because I know it's not true. The fact they're offended? It means I hit too close to home! And what can they do anyway? Cancel me? I'm not even on the Internet. And look, my book sales are completely unaffected. We're doing fine!

"Yes, it's selling, but... Amazon is also mad, and they've frozen your royalties!"

Wh-What!? What did you say? My... MY ROYALTIES!? Are you kidding me!? Amazon did what!?

"Yes! They said you won't get paid until you apologize and you fix your content! Are you really sure that's okay?"

WHAT?! I... Dammit!... Alright, fine. I'll say something! Everyone, pay attention, get ready for the final lesson!

Afterword

11

TRUE COURAGE VS. TOXIC COURAGE

First of all, I'd like to issue an apology. I'm sorry I made many readers feel uncomfortable. This should never have happened, and there is no excuse for what I did. I'm also sorry for taking so long to apologize, it's been a difficult week.

Over the past week, I've been harassed, I've received death threats, I called the police. My fiancée was stalked and had an emotional breakdown. Our adopted daughter cried every night to sleep, she kept asking us. "Why? Mom? Dad? Why do these people on the Internet hate us so much?" And we have no response. Because... we knew deep down we were in the wrong. And all your anger towards us is justified.

So I'm not saying this to gain sympathy. The truth is quite the opposite. I'm glad I've been taught this lesson. Because... I need to be taught that our actions have consequences in life. And... you know... I feel humbled. When people from the other side reached out to me, and patiently told me their sides of the story... oh my, what a humiliating experience that was.

So I mustered up my courage and decided to make this apology. Because true courage is about owning up to your mistakes. Would I have preferred I made no mistakes, ever? No. Because that means not putting myself in situations where I can learn and improve. This has been a great learning experience for me, and I appreciate that you put me through this.

Can we separate the art from the artist?

I would argue yes. Someone asked me a very thoughtful question once. "Do you really think a healthy and normal person would've written *Crime and Punishment*? Or *Notes from the Underground*?"

He had a point. Because, truth be told, as I read Dostoevsky's work, this is clearly not someone happy, or even normal. This is someone disturbed. Depressed. With a lot of dark thoughts. Most people who know him in real life would probably consider him "awful."

But in some sense, I think we should thank him, for being depressed, for engaging in all these disturbing thoughts. He suffered by living that awful life, so he could enrich our lives by bestowing the world with all these timeless literary classics.

When we really look into his mind, what does he need? He doesn't need you to judge him… He needs help. So let's be kind. That's why diversity is strength. And that's what us truly human.

I finally decided to see therapy

I criticized psychology. But after a conversation with a reader who is a psychologist... I changed my mind. I realized they're really just very nice people. He just wanted to have a conversation. And he just wanted to help.

I remember what he said to me, *"Professor, when you call someone an 'idiot,' it just sounds like you're projecting your own insecurities onto others, as a defense mechanism to overcompensate for your inferiority complex. So you actually deserve to be sympathized, not criticized."*

I... I guess you're right.

"Yes, and when you dislike psychologists so much? It doesn't feel like an intellectual critique, it feels like a personal one. You... you were bullied when you were younger, weren't you? Maybe you were... you were hurt by psychologists? Were... were you abused? That would explain everything. All your criticism? It was actually your way of seizing back control. It's the only coping mechanism you know to deal with your deep-seated trauma."

Wow... I think you're right again. I guess there is no use hiding it anymore. When I was younger, I was indeed abused... I was sexually assaulted by psychologists... I'm sorry, I don't feel comfortable getting into the story now. I tried so hard to forget it for so many years.

But then again, it sounds silly, doesn't it? Because that was many, many years ago. Since then, psychology as a field has improved by a lot. I just hope... maybe it's a selfish hope, but I hope there is more change.

"That's alright, Professor. But that's exactly why spreading awareness of psychology is so important."

I completely agree... You know, I'm not going to ask for forgiveness, because I don't deserve it. I want to apologize with my action, not my words. That's why I'm going to donate 90% of my book's earnings to the Psychology Research Foundation.

Right now my earning is frozen, but I hope Amazon would do the right thing and unfreeze it. As things stand, they're just going to use the money to make some billionaire richer. But I want to make a real social impact.

I can't change the past, but I can make sure I never make such mistakes again in the future. And I ask you to give me a chance to make it right again. Allow me to prove it to you that I have indeed changed. I owe you this much.

And with that, dear reader, I'd like to conclude this book. I appreciate you, and I appreciate the journey we've been through together. All the best.

R.M.

Dedication

Professor Raymond Marylowe would like to thank Dan S. Kennedy. Without him, this book would not have been written.

About The Author

If you have questions, you can send one question per book purchase to professor@raymondmarylowe.com. Attach a selfie of you holding this book (physical book or on your kindle device) so the question will be forward to Prof. Marylowe, and he will reply.

www.ingramcontent.com/pod-product-compliance
Lightning Source LLC
Chambersburg PA
CBHW071248070526
44583CB00017B/2372